STOIC ETHICS

Also Available from Bloomsbury

Aristotle's Ethics, Hope May
Aristotle's Theory of Knowledge, Thomas Kiefer
Aristotle, Ethics and Pleasure, Michael Weinman
Cicero's Ethics, Harald Thorsrud
Happiness and Greek Ethical Thought, Andrew Holowchak
Plato's Stepping Stones, Michael Cormack
The Ideas of Socrates, Matthew S. Linck

STOIC ETHICS

Epictetus and Happiness as Freedom

William O. Stephens
Creighton University, USA

Bloomsbury Academic
An imprint of Bloomsbury Publishing Plc

B L O O M S B U R Y
LONDON · OXFORD · NEW YORK · NEW DELHI · SYDNEY

Bloomsbury Academic
An imprint of Bloomsbury Publishing Plc

50 Bedford Square	1385 Broadway
London	New York
WC1B 3DP	NY 10018
UK	USA

www.bloomsbury.com

BLOOMSBURY and the Diana logo are trademarks of Bloomsbury Publishing Plc

First published in Great Britain 2007
Paperback edition first published 2017

Copyright © William O. Stephens, 2007, 2018

Marilyn Dunn has asserted her right under the Copyright, Designs and Patents
Act, 1988, to be identified as Author of this work.

For legal purposes the Acknowledgements on p. vii constitute an
extension of this copyright page.

British Library Cataloguing-in-Publication Data
A catalogue record for this book is available from the British Library.

ISBN: HB: 978-0-8264-9608-9
PB: 978-1-3500-6835-3
ePDF: 978-1-4411-8791-8
ePub: 978-1-4411-7045-3

Library of Congress Cataloguing-in-Publication Data
A catalog record for this book is available from the Library of Congress.

Series: Bloomsbury Studies in Ancient Philosophy

Typeset by Fakenham Photosetting, Fakenham, Norfolk

To find out more about our authors and books visit www.bloomsbury.com
and sign up for our newsletters.

Contents

Foreword

This is a lightly edited version of my 1990 doctoral dissertation at the University of Pennsylvania supervised by Professor Charles H. Kahn titled *Stoic Strength: An Examination of the Ethics of Epictetus*. After leaving Penn, I turned to other projects at Creighton without a serious thought to seek a publisher for the largest early relic of my years of fascination with Epictetus. On 15 September 2004 Dr Jim Fieser of the Philosophy Department at the University of Tennessee at Martin emailed me with that very thought. Without his prompting, encouragement, and persistence, this monograph would have been fated to remain undisturbed, collecting dust in the archives of University Microfilms International in Ann Arbor, as it were, perched precariously above the dustbin of history. Readers will judge whether publishing this dissertation is a case of the old cliché 'Better late than never.'

Technologically speaking, 1990 was an age ago. The manuscript was produced using a Magnavox Videowriter and an IBM correcting Selectric typewriter with a Greek font element. Email was unknown. Yet Epictetus' gritty charm endures. So the bibliography has been updated to include selected publications after 1990 in which Epictetus figures prominently, but not work in Stoic ethics broadly. My hope is that others may find this monograph as useful as Jim believes it is. I dedicate this dusted-off package, retitled to please my publisher, to him. I also again thank my colleagues at Penn for their generous comments and support offered long ago.

August 2006
WOS

Abbreviations

D.L.   Hicks, R. D. (1925, 1972 repr.) (tr.), *Diogenes Laertius: Lives of Eminent Philosophers*. 2 vols. Loeb Classical Library. London: W. Heinemann.

NE   Aristotle, *Nicomachean Ethics*, in W. D. Ross and J. A. Smith (1908–52) (trs), *The Works of Aristotle*. Oxford: Clarendon Press.

ENCH   *Encheridion* = *Handook*. The *Discourses* are cited by book, chapter, and section, and the *Encheridion* by chapter and section

SE AM   Mutschmann, H. and Mau, J. (1961) (eds), *Sexti Empirici Opera, vols II and III Adversus Mathematicos*. Leipzig: Teubner.

SVF   Arnim, H. von, *Stoicorum Veterum Fragmenta*. Vols 1–3 (1903–05), Vol. 4 (1924), indexes by M. Adler. Leipzig: Teubner.

Ēthos anthrōpōi daimōn.
'A person's character is his fate.'

Herakleitos

Es ist die Sache der Wenigsten, unabhängig zu sein:—es ist ein
Vorrecht der Starken.
'It is the concern of extremely few to be independent: – it is a
privilege of the strong.'

F. W. Nietzsche

Preface

A quick sketch of the last twelve decades of scholarship on Epictetus can provide a bit of orientation. The German giant of Epictetus studies was Bonhöffer (1890, 1894, 1911). He remains the only author of not two but three volumes on our philosopher. The contributions of subsequent German scholars have been much more modest in scope.[1] Work in French has also been steady, though not voluminous.[2] Epictetus has received the attention of a few Italians[3] and one Pole.[4] But in the last nine years several excellent contributions[5] have joined earlier work in English.[6] So these are good times for studying Epictetus. I hope that this study provides a sufficiently fresh approach to understanding the character of his style of teaching Stoic wisdom.

Epictetus was born the son of a slave woman in Hierapolis in Phrygia[7] some time between 50 and 60 CE.[8] His lameness and period of enslavement undoubtedly contributed to the development of his conception of happiness as freedom.[9] This freedom is not bodily, financial, or political, but rather the only freedom which can, if the individual musters sufficient self-discipline and self-determination, never be lost. It is freedom of the mind, freedom of assent, desire, and volition. Though a person's body can, because of its nature, belong to another, Epictetus' resolute conviction was that one's mind is always one's own. Like Socrates, Epictetus believed that to do philosophy was to *live* as a philosopher.[10] For both men this art of living consisted in determining what the philosopher must know in order to judge and act correctly.

It was during the time he was owned by Nero's freedman and administrative secretary Epaphroditus that Epictetus took lessons from the great Stoic teacher of the day, C. Musonius Rufus. Oldfather claims that

[s]o many passages in Epictetus can be paralleled closely from the remaining fragments of Rufus (as Epictetus always calls him) that there can be *no doubt* but the system of thought in the pupil is little more than an echo, with changes of emphasis due to the personal equation, of that of the master.[11]

Sandbach observes that Rufus 'makes some use of the denial that anything indifferent is good or bad: the proofs of this should, he says, constantly be repeated; it is a truth which demonstrates that exile cannot rob a man of anything really good'.[12] Moreover, the emphasis on the necessity of an austere and frugal lifestyle is certainly shared by both the master and his pupil.

Epictetus was among the philosophers expelled from Rome by the emperor Domitian (presumably in 89 or 92 CE). He moved to Nicopolis in Epirus and founded a school in order to promulgate the ideas of Stoicism. The four books entitled *Arrian's Discourses of Epictetus* are generally believed to be not the transcripts of the formal readings of Stoic disquisitions, but rather Epictetus' expositions of particular issues from those readings and practically oriented responses to his students' recitations given to them in less formal seminars.[13] Their purpose, evidently, is to encourage, advise, and exhort his pupils to learn to apply Stoic ideas. Flavius Arrianus was one of the young Romans who attended Epictetus' classes. His brief compilation of the *Diatribae* called the *Encheiridion* ('Manual' or 'Handbook') has, relative to its modest size, exercised a disproportionately large impact on the subsequent thought of European intellectuals. I quite agree with Sherman that although the *Diatribae* and the *Encheiridion* are secondary sources since they were composed by the student Arrian and not by the teacher himself, 'as sources they lie much closer to the time and teaching of the Stoic philosophy than any others.'[14] As to the question of the accuracy of Arrian's reporting of Epictetus' lectures, I concur with De Lacy that

[w]e need only assume that Epictetus had a systematic ethics which he taught in his school and which Arrian used for a framework in the first book of the *Discourses*. In spite of his

literary imitation of Xenophon, Arrian has portrayed in detail the methods and subjects of Epictetus' teaching. It is not unlikely, therefore, that the plan of Arrian's work is based on Epictetus' system of ethics.[15]

Seneca's writings are interesting in themselves yet sometimes lack the earnest spirit of Stoicism so evident in Epictetus' *Discourses*. Seneca's life and personal practices fell far short of the austere Stoic ethics he preached,[16] and this disingenuous subtext is reflected in his writing. *The Meditations to Myself* of the emperor Marcus Aurelius, on the other hand, lack the hypocrisy of a Seneca, but they also lack the fervent optimism of Epictetus' *Discourses*.[17] Marcus is primarily concerned with consoling himself, whereas Epictetus' interest is not a private one. The former slave turned teacher makes a concerted effort to instill the doctrine of Stoicism in his students by urgently reminding them that they must persistently and rationally *apply* what they learn in the classroom to every situation of their daily lives.

In short, if we observe, we shall find mankind distressed by nothing so much as by the irrational, and again attracted to nothing so much as to the rational. Now it so happens that the rational and the irrational are different for different persons, precisely as good and evil, and the profitable and the unprofitable, are different for different persons. It is for this especially that we need education, so as to learn how, in conformity with nature, to adapt to specific instances our preconceived idea of what is rational and what is irrational. But for determining the rational and the irrational, we employ not only our estimates of the value of external things, but also the criterion of that which is in keeping with one's character. (1.2.4–7)[18]

Epictetus does not hesitate to castigate himself when his behavior diverges from the disciplined regimen called for by his understanding of Stoic principles. For these reasons I believe Epictetus provides us with the best available source for the spirit and content of Roman Stoicism expressed in a sincere, moving, and frank style.

These are the considerations that motivate my examination of the ethics of Epictetus.

Notes

1. Schweingruber (1943), Capelle (1948), Barth (1951), Spanneut (1962, 1972), Wirth (1967), Döring (1974), Štajerman (1975), Billerbeck (1978), Gretenkord (1981). Wehner (2000) is reviewed by Stephens (2003).

2. The only book-length examination is Colardeau (1903). Shorter papers include Bosshard (1929), Jagu (1946), Angers (1954), Cadou (1954), Le Hir (1954), Germain (1964), Moreau (1964), Moulinier (1964), Bodson (1967), Cizek (1975), Hadot (1978), and Nakhov (1980).

3. Pesce (1939), Martinazzoli (1948), Riondato (1965), Laurenti (1966), Decleva Caizzi (1977).

4. Szumska (1964).

5. Dobbin (1991, 1998), Inwood (1996), Kamtekar (1998), Boter (1999), and most of all Long (2002), which is reviewed by Stephens (2003).

6. De Lacy (1943), Starr (1949), Bonforte (1955), Hijmans (1959), Kokolakis (1961), Millar (1965), Dudley (1967), Xenakis (1968, 1969), Stanton (1968), Brunt (1977), Dragona-Monachou (1978–79).

7. Oldfather makes much of this in his introduction to the Loeb Classical Library edition of Epictetus: 'From of old the Phrygians had conceived of their deities with a singular intensity and entered into their worship with a passion that was often fanaticism, and sometimes downright frenzy. It is, therefore, not unnatural that the one Greek philosopher who, despite the monistic and necessitarian postulates of his philosophy, conceived of his God in as vivid a fashion as the writers of the New Testament, and almost as intimately as the founder of Christianity himself, should have inherited the passion for a personal god from the folk and land of his nativity' (Oldfather, 1925: viii).

8. Reale (1990: 468).

9. Oldfather writes: 'The tone and temper of his whole life were determined thereby. An all-engulfing passion for independence and freedom so preoccupied him in his youth, that throughout his life he was obsessed with the fear of restraint, and tended to regard mere liberty, even in its negative aspect alone, as almost the highest conceivable good' (Oldfather, 1925: vii–viii).

10. See Long (2002) for a detailed examination of Epictetus' debt to Plato's Socrates.

11. Oldfather, 1925: viii n. 2; my emphasis. I am skeptical of Oldfather's certainty exactly because only a few fragments of Rufus are extant. I would grant Epictetus some originality, for example, in what is evidently an innovative use of *prohairesis* as an early idea of the self.

12. Sandbach (1975).

13. Note, for example, the remarks of Otto Halbauer, *De diatribis Epicteti*, Leipzig (1911), p. 56 quoted by Oldfather: 'The *Diatribae* are not the curriculum proper, nor even a part of that curriculum. On the contrary, this consisted of readings from the Stoic writings, while the *Diatribae* accompany the formal instruction, dwell on this point or on that, which Epictetus regarded as of special importance, above all give him an opportunity for familiar discourse with his pupils, and for discussing with them in a friendly spirit their personal affairs' (Oldfather, 1925: xv).

14. Sherman (1967: 33).

15. De Lacy (1943: 113). On the authorship of the *Discourses*, I side with Long (2002: 38–43 and 64–5) and against Dobbin (1998: xx–xxiii).

16. See Seneca (1958: 6–9).

17. For greater elaboration on Marcus' somberness see Stephens (2005 and 1998).

18. The standard edition of *Arrian's Discourses of Epictetus* is Schenkl (1916). I generally follow Oldfather's translation (1925–28) but often modify it, sometimes significantly. The *Discourses* are cited by book, chapter, and section, and the *Encheiridion* by chapter and section.

Introduction

While Aristotle held that virtue alone is not a sufficient condition for *eudaimonia* since some external goods are definitely also necessary,[1] there was another strong trend in ancient Greek ethical thought originating in Socrates and passing down through Antisthenes, the Cynics, and on to the Hellenistic philosophers that strongly emphasized self-sufficiency (*autarkeia*). This trend, contrary to the Aristotelian view, held that a certain kind of internal state of the soul is not only a sufficient condition of *eudaimonia*, but is moreover its only condition. 'Hellenistic philosophers shared a general interest in completely internalizing happiness; their project was to make happiness depend essentially on the agent's moral character and beliefs, and thus to minimize or discount its dependence on external contingencies.'[2] The belief that happiness is living in agreement with nature, and that this consists in achieving a virtuous character that in no way relies upon moral luck or fortune (and hence material circumstances), is the characteristic feature of Cynicism and Stoicism.

Orthodox Stoicism, as represented by Zeno, the founder of the school, and Chrysippus, the great systematizer of the early Stoa, maintained that only the virtues (*aretai*), prudence, justice, courage, moderation, etc. are strictly 'good' (*agathon*), since they and they alone under all conditions always benefit and never harm us (D.L. 7.101–3). Vice (*kakia*), foolishness, injustice, etc. were, conversely, considered the only truly 'bad' thing (*kakon*) (D.L. 7.101–3) since these things are the only things harmful to us under all conditions, and therefore are necessarily productive of unhappiness (*kakodaimonia*). All things lying in the non-moral sphere, health, wealth, reputation, strength, and the like, the Stoics termed 'indifferents' (*adiaphora*) and labeled 'neutral' (*oudetera*) since they were neither good nor bad strictly speaking and it is possible to be happy (*eudaimōn*) without them (*SVF* 3.104). Yet, while virtue was thus unconditionally good and vice unconditionally evil, they further divided the class of indifferents into those which are 'preferred' (*proēgmena*) and were provisionally, conditionally 'choiceworthy' or 'valuable' (*axia*), and those which are 'dispreferred' (*apoproēgmena*) and were provisionally, conditionally 'unchoiceworthy' or 'valueless' (*apaxia*) (*SVF* 3.128). The indifferents which are 'to-be-taken' are the ones in accordance with nature (*ta kata phusin*) e.g. health, strength, well-functioning sense organs and the like. The indifferents which are 'contrary to nature' (*ta para phusin*) are 'not-to-be-taken' (*SVF* 3.124).

> Value [*axia*] has three senses: a thing's contribution and merit per se, the expert's appraisal, and thirdly, what Antipater calls 'selective': according to this when circumstances permit, we choose these particular things instead of those, for instance health instead of disease, life instead of death, wealth instead of poverty.[3]

So for orthodox Stoicism life, health, wealth, beauty, strength, *et al.*, though morally indifferent (since they do not in themselves contribute to the happy, healthy, and virtuous state of the *psyche*) were, *ceteris paribus*, seen to have practical worth. Death, disease, poverty, ugliness, weakness, and the like were similarly seen to be indifferents which were ordinarily to be avoided. If, however, circumstances were such that selecting them was necessary in order to preserve one's honor, dignity, and moral integrity, then they *must* be selected.

The decisive importance of the circumstances surrounding an action is most prominent in the position of Aristo of Chios. He rejected all distinctions within the class of 'indifferents' and so was considered a heretic for this heterodoxy.

> Aristo of Chios denied that health and everything similar to it is a preferred indifferent. For to call it a preferred indifferent is equivalent to judging it a good, and different practically in name alone. For without exception things indifferent as between virtue

and vice have no difference at all, nor are some of them preferred by nature while others are dispreferred, but in the face of the different circumstances of the occasions neither those which are said to be preferred prove to be unconditionally preferred, nor are those said to be dispreferred of necessity dispreferred. For if healthy men had to serve a tyrant and be destroyed for this reason, while the sick had to be released from the service and, therewith also from destruction, the wise man would rather choose sickness in this circumstance than health. Thus neither is health unconditionally preferred nor sickness dispreferred. Just as in writing people's names we put different letters first at different times, *adapting them to the different circumstances* not because some letters are given priority over others by nature but because the circumstances *compel* us to do this, so too in the things which are between virtue and vice no natural priority for some over others arises but a priority which is based rather on circumstances.[4]

Aristo's formulation of the end was, '... to live with a disposition of indifference towards what is intermediate between vice and virtue, not retaining any difference at all within that class of things, but *being equally disposed towards them all.*'[5] One is equally disposed towards all 'externals' in a way similar to the way one is equally disposed to all letters of the alphabet. The knowledge of the virtuous agent is thus akin to the knowledge of the grammarian. It is this conditionality of the value of 'indifferents' which leads Aristo to deny them any intrinsic worth.

As is clear from the two passages above, Aristo lays all emphasis on the situational, circumstantial context of occasions for action. This second passage from Diogenes Laertius ends with a very suggestive simile: 'For the wise man is like the good actor who, whether he puts on the mask of Thersites or Agamemnon, plays either part in the proper way.'[6] This is the very same simile Epictetus uses in *Ench.* 17 (and cf. *Ench.* 37), and it represents a significant parallel between Aristo and Epictetus. In any case, Aristo insists that it is these practical circumstances which dictate the proper employment of things, not any illusory intrinsic nature of the things themselves.[7]

Since Epictetus so emphatically repeats that externals are not the Stoic's concern since they do not belong to us, it is tempting to see him close to accepting Aristo's denial of intrinsic, non-moral value. Wealth, strength, beauty, health, popularity, and the like may be putative goods, but since their loss cannot rob one of any real 'good' (*agathon*), intrinsically they have mere 'worth' (*axia*) because they are *morally* indifferent. They are not good as means, but are rather choiceworthy as natural.

Although the orthodox view grants that something which can be used badly is not something 'good' (i.e. health and wealth can be used to do harm), unlike Aristo, Zeno and Chrysippus held that the proper attitude toward *ta kata phusin* was not unqualified indifference but knowledge of how they should be used since 'the manner of using them is constitutive of happiness or unhappiness' (D.L. 7.104; *SVF* 3.104).

As Long and Sedley suggest, Epictetus' constant insistence on making correct use of *phantasiai* may be viewed as a later, expanded version of this doctrine.[8] I maintain in Chapter 1 that although in emphasis Epictetus may seem to follow Aristo in the heterodox rejection of the division of indifferents into 'preferred' and 'dispreferred,' Epictetus in fact follows his teacher Musonius on this point. I am inclined to concur with Bonhöffer that Epictetus implicitly assumes the orthodox distinction.[9] Epictetus wants to highlight the simple division between 'things up to me' and 'things not up to me' in order to confine all good and evil to the former.

In Chapter 2, I illustrate how Epictetus elaborates on how the use of 'externals' is not morally neutral (thus further developing the earlier view of Zeno and Chrysippus), although the 'externals' per se are certainly not of unconditional value. 'Is health a good, and illness an evil? No, man. What then? To be well for a good end is good, to be well for an evil end is evil' (3.26.38). In passages like this we can see how Epictetus' account of 'indifferents' is intended both to preserve consistency by denying unconditional, i.e. moral, value to externals, *and* to frame suitably the early Stoic intuition that as long as the ends for which externals are used are indubitably virtuous, *ceteris paribus*, it is rational and natural to select health over illness, pleasure over pain, beauty over ugliness, and so on.

Epictetus holds the traditional Stoic view that happiness is living according to nature, and that for human beings this essentially consists in living according to reason. What distinctly characterizes Epictetus' Stoicism, however, is that this life according to reason involves both (1) consistently making the correct judgement about what lies within one's power and what does not, i.e. where one's good is located, and (2) deciding what the appropriate attitude or action to be adopted is in particular circumstances, i.e. the correct judgement as to what belongs to one's role in these circumstances (*to kathēkon*). This, for Epictetus, is what getting an education means.

In Chapter 3, I discuss how the Stoic deals with other people by showing them sympathy and pity without thereby letting sufferers' *pathē* ensnare her own emotional freedom. People are thus exclusively a source of love and joy for the Stoic sage. It is because of his knowledge of good and evil that only the wise person has the power to love.

In my final chapter, I expound Epictetus' teleology of nature in order to scrutinize the theoretical underpinnings of his conception of happiness (*eudaimonia*) as imperturbability (*ataraxia*) in the form of mental and emotional freedom (*eleutheria*). I conclude with my assessment of the overall strengths and weaknesses of Epictetus' moral psychology and the potential of Stoic ethics.

Notes

1 This is most explicit at *NE* 1099b26–8: 'Of the remaining (i.e. external) goods, *some must necessarily pre-exist as conditions of happiness*, and others are naturally co-operative and useful as instruments' (Ross tr., my emphasis). Cf. also *NE* 1097b15–16, 1099a31–2, 1099b7, and the pronouncement at 1101a15–16: he is 'happy who is in accordance with complete virtue and is *sufficiently equipped with external goods*' (Ross tr., my emphasis).
2 Long (1996: 30).
3 Long and Sedley's translation of *SVF* 3.124; Long and Sedley (1987: Vol. 1, 355).

4   Long and Sedley's translation of *SE AM* 11.64–7 (*SVF* 1.361), my
    emphasis; Long and Sedley (1987: Vol. 1, 355–6).
5   Long and Sedley's translation of D.L. 7.160; my emphasis.
6   *Ibid.*
7   For a study of Aristo of Chios, see Ioppolo (1980).
8   Long and Sedley (1987: Vol. 1, 359).
9   Bonhöffer (1894: 43).

Chapter 1

What exactly is 'up to me'[1]?

A. Internals VS. externals

The basic empirical observation which forms the foundation of Epictetus' ethical system is that some things are up to us while others are not up to us.[2] Although this observation initially strikes us as obvious and simple-minded, Epictetus will use it to draw several quite profound conclusions about rational action. By 'up to us' Epictetus seems to mean that we are entirely free to determine these things as we will; there are no forces external to us which determine these things against our wishes. These things which are 'up to us' include *hypolēpsis* (conception/opinion), *hormē* (impulse-to-choose), *orexis* (desire), *ekklisis* (aversion), 'and in a word all that is our own doing.'[3] At 1.4.11 he elaborates on this last phrase in connection with *orexis, ekklisis,* and *hormē* by saying that in desire and aversion one's *ergon* (work/doing) is to get what you desire and escape what you would avoid, in impulse-to-choose (and refusal) to commit no fault, and not to be being deceived in giving and withholding assent. The use of *phantasiai*[4] is also up to us,[5] and in fact he indicates that the *dunamis* (capacity) which makes use of *phantasiai* is one and the same with the *dunamis* of choice and refusal, of desire and aversion (1.1.12).[6] This *dunamis* is *logos* (reason). Epictetus says that reason is given to us by nature for the proper use of *phantasiai* (1.20.5) and that the ability to use sense-impressions rationally (i.e. in accordance with nature and perfectly) is what distinguishes us as human beings, our superiority over other animals lying in our reason (3.1.25–6). At the moment they occur, *phantasiai* are not voluntary, they simply affect the mind. They are not effluences from physical objects. Rather, *phantasiai* are conceptual constructs of the mind. The hormetic representation, when assented to, forms the 'impulse to choose,' i.e. the impulse to act, and is voluntary. This is what Epictetus is referring to when he insists we use *phantasiai* correctly.

The things not up to us are 'the body, the parts of the body, possessions, parents, brothers, children, country, in a word all that with which we associate',[7] our reputation, public office, and, in a word, all that is not our own doing (*Ench.* 1.1). Now Epictetus classifies all these things as not 'up to us' or 'under our control' because they are not *completely* under our control nor are they *at all times* under our control. This is because by their very nature they are weak, slavish, subject to hindrance, and not our own (*Ench.* 1.2). This is not to say that we can have no effect whatsoever on any of these 'externals', nor that they should be totally ignored. Rather, the idea is simply that the first group (which for ease of reference I will often call 'internals'[8]) contains things which are by their nature free, unhindered, and unimpeded (*Ench.* 1.2).

Now to the reader it will not be at all obvious how *hormē* and *orexis* are 'up to us.' Epictetus tacitly follows the traditional Stoic doctrine that there are two orders of value. The following table illustrates the distinctions operative in Epictetus:

Type of Value	*Object is*
(Pro)hairetic	unconditionally good; good as means for producing happiness
Eclectic	conditionally valuable; choiceworthy as intrinsically natural

Our desires (*orexeis*) are for things we take to be goods (*agatha*), our aversions (*ekkliseis*) are for things we take to be evils (*kaka*). As a Stoic, Epictetus limits good and evil to the moral value and disvalue of the soul. Specifically, he contends that only the virtues are strictly good, and only the vices are strictly evil. Only in the moral sphere is there hairetic value. Everything else is 'indifferent' because it has no moral value. Yet some 'indifferents' will have non-moral value (*axia*) and others will have non-moral disvalue (*apaxia*). If an object is worth selecting for pragmatic reasons, for example, then it has eclectic value. For the Stoics 'goods' and 'evils' are different not in degree but in kind from 'choiceworthy' and 'unchoiceworthy' items. I will discuss the status of the value of material objects at length in Chapter 2. Epictetus insists we are responsible for our *orexeis* because when we have a real desire for, say, a cake, and thus have an impulse to act (to have the cake), it is because we are conceiving of the cake as being good (*agathon*). This is precisely to misunderstand the nature of the cake and to misjudge its inherent value.

For Epictetus, making the distinction between the things 'up to us' and the things 'not up to us' is no trivial task. Rather, it is what getting an education means (1.22.9). He says 'to be getting an education means this: to be learning what is your own, and what is another's' (4.5.7). That the things 'up to me' are obviously one and the same as 'what is my own' just as the things 'not up to me' are not mine and so are another's is clear from 3.24.3: 'The things that are subject to hindrance, deprivation, and compulsion are not a man's own, but those which cannot be hindered are his own.' Epictetus says that this is the knowledge with which Antisthenes set Diogenes free:

> How did Antisthenes set him free? Listen to what Diogenes says, 'He taught me what was mine, and what was not mine. Property is not mine; kinsmen, members of my household, friends, reputation, familiar places, converse with men – all these are not my own. 'What, then, *is* yours? Power to deal with external impressions.' He showed me that I possess this beyond all hindrance and constraint; no one can hamper me; no one can force me to deal with them otherwise than as I will.' (3.24.68–9; cf. 1.1.21)

Clearly, then, the things 'up to me,' the things which are 'my own,' and 'internals' are all one and the same group.

Given this fundamental division of things in the world, Epictetus maintains we have an equally fundamental choice to make. We can place the good amongst internals and then desire and attend to them as good, or we can place the good amongst externals and desire and pursue then as good. Because of the nature of each group, the only rational choice according to Epictetus is to place the good exclusively within internals and limit one's desires to them.

> If you do not wish to desire[9] without failing to get, or to avoid without falling into the object of your aversion, desire none of those things which are not your own, and avoid none of those things which are not under your control. If not, you are of necessity bound to fail in achieving your desires, and to fall into what you would avoid.[10]

The Stoic knows why good things (agatha) are good, why bad things (*kaka*) are bad, and why the things indifferent are neither good nor bad. The cake no longer impresses itself upon the adult Stoic as an ineluctably tempting goody[11] as it did in his childhood. The *phantasiai* of rational beings are rational *phantasiai;* that is why they are of an essentially different kind from the *phantasiai* of non-rational beings like human children and non-human animals.

From the passage quoted above we see the first reason Epictetus finds the desire for externals to be irrational – success in acquiring them is, by their nature, never guaranteed. Hence, to want to have the things not up to you is to subject your desires to luck, contingency, and compulsion. Epictetus thinks that to endanger the fulfillment of your desires is needless. Yet, he explains, 'If you always bear in mind what is your own and what is another's, you will never be disturbed' (2.6.8) since, he assumes, this will prompt you to limit your desire to the former group. Thus the first reason for not desiring externals is the unavoidable difficulty involved in acquiring them and the inevitable frustration that results from that difficulty.

A second reason Epictetus gives for not considering externals good seems to be that it is much more difficult to manage many things (externals) than to concentrate our attention on only one thing (the faculty which makes use of sense-impressions):

But now, although it is in our power to care for one thing only and devote ourselves to but one, we choose rather to care for many things, and to be tied fast to many, even to our body and our estate and brother and friend and child and slave. Wherefore, being tied fast to many things, we are burdened and dragged down by them. (1.1.14–15)

The idea seems to be that trouble can arise with any one of these many externals and this worry bogs us down in the business of managing them all.[12] To worry about an external is to sacrifice one's peace of mind in the false belief that that external is a good which contributes to one's happiness.

This may be the weakest reason Epictetus offers for not valuing externals. We can easily imagine that some shrewd capitalist could be quite adept at managing his material wealth and possessions.[13] Not only could such a wealthy lover of possessions hire assistants to help him handle his material affairs so as to avoid being 'burdened and dragged down by them,' but he might even derive positive exhilaration from juggling his plethora of possessions. Epictetus would deny that this 'exhilaration' would be true *eudaimonia* since, I imagine, it would involve a mental busy-ness which would detract from rather than add to peace of mind.

A third reason for not placing the good in externals is that our losses and pains have to do only with our possessions (1.18.16). Material possessions can be lost, broken, or, like Epictetus' iron lamp in 1.18.15, stolen. Thus if one admires a material thing, then one will be angry when it is lost.

For, mark you, stop admiring your clothes, and you are not angry at the man who steals them; stop admiring your wife's beauty, and you are not angry at her adulterer. Know that a thief or an adulterer has no place among the things that are your own, but only among the things that are another's and that are not under your control. If you give these things up and count them as nothing, at whom have you still ground to feel angry? (1.18.11–12)

Here the idea is twofold. If one ceases to admire an external, then one will not be upset with its loss, nor will one feel angry toward the person or persons responsible for its loss. But since clothes can be stolen, and a wife's fidelity can be lost, these and all other externals are never secure even if one does succeed in obtaining them. Even health and a sound body (cf. 1.22.12) are not to be considered goods since they can be lost by way of disease or physical pain.

That Epictetus follows the orthodox acceptance of the non-moral value of those indifferents which are ordinarily, conditionally, and instrumentally worth selecting is evident from this passage: 'Therefore Chrysippus well says, "As long as the consequences are not clear to me, I cleave ever to what is better adapted to secure those things that are in accordance with nature; for God has created me with the faculty of selecting things (*ekletikon*)"' (2.6.8–9). God has made Epictetus so as to be happy. Ordinarily exercise and a good diet make Epictetus healthy, and so happy. Consequently, Epictetus has a provisionally good reason for selecting food and activities that tend to make him healthy. 'But if I really knew that it was ordained for me to be ill at this present moment, I would even be impelled toward illness; for the foot also if it had a mind, would be impelled toward being covered with mud' (2.6.10). This is why even bodily health is only conditionally valuable (*axia*), not unconditionally good.

What, then, is the Stoic's attitude toward bodily pleasure and pain? When I stub my toe I experience irritation (*ponos*). When I choose to get mad about stubbing my toe I suffer, that is to say I subject myself to pain (*lupē*). Pleasure (*hēdonē*) is not of any hairetic value, so it is indifferent. Yet *ceteris paribus* pleasure will in fact be selectable (*eklektikon* / *proēgmenon*) as 'choiceworthy,' *axia*, though never as 'good,' *agathon*.

A fourth reason Epictetus gives for not placing the good among externals is the hostile competition and turmoil which ensue from everyone contending for the same externals.

Where, then, shall we place 'the good'? To what class of things are we going to apply it? To the class of things that are under our control? – What, is not health, then, a good thing, and a sound body, and life? Nay, and not even children, or parents, or country? – And who will tolerate you if you deny that? Therefore, let us transfer the designation 'good' to these things. But is it possible, then, for a man to be happy if he sustains injury and fails to get that which is good? – It is not possible. – And to maintain the proper relations with his associates? And how can it be possible? For it is my nature to look out for my own interest. If it is my interest to have a farm, it is my interest to take it away from my neighbour; if it is my interest to have a cloak, it is my interest also to steal it from a bath. This is the source of wars, seditions, tyrannies, plots. (1.22.11–14)

The reasoning here is that if externals are judged good, then they will be desired and each individual will do whatever is necessary in order to have them. Since presumably there is always a limited supply of these externals around, Epictetus infers that out of self-interest people will compete vigorously against one another by plotting, scheming, stealing, and fighting in order to get what they desire. Thus Epictetus holds that considering externals as goods will eliminate all scruples pertaining to how such goods are acquired. Coupled with the natural drive to look out for one's own interest, this valuation becomes the root cause of virtually all social and political conflict.

When Epictetus claims above that 'it is my nature to look out for my own interest (*to emon sumpheron*)' he is reformulating in different words the traditional Stoic idea that self-preservation is the object of any animal's (including a human being's) first impulse (D.L. 7.85). Thus Epictetus is quite consistent with orthodox Stoicism in holding that self-interest is a brute fact of human (and animal) nature. It is important to note that, in contrast, he certainly does not view the desire for externals to be an unchangeable element of human nature. Epictetus consistently insists that the motive of our actions, of our utterances, of our being elated, of our being depressed, of our avoiding things, and of our pursuing things, is not beyond our control. Rather, the cause of every action an agent performs is his wanting to do so (1.11.28–30). We are responsible for our desires since our impulses to act, as rational adults, stem from what we conceive of as being good. It is the old impulses to desire externals like cake as good which were habituated into us as children that we must overcome as adults. Consequently, the tenacious pursuit of externals is in Epictetus' view the result of a mistaken choice, a misestimation of where the good truly lies. To place the good amongst externals is once again contrary to reason because doing so directly leads us to compete viciously and struggle violently with each other for these externals. This can predictably escalate into anarchic, social chaos. The rational alternative, as Epictetus sees it, is to place the good only amongst our (internal) virtues and thereby avert such overwhelming strife.

The fifth, and for Epictetus probably the most important, reason for the individual not to desire externals is that to pursue externals necessarily requires sacrificing one's own moral worth and dignity, i.e. what is truly one's own.

> You cannot wish for a consulship and at the same time wish for this; you cannot have set your heart upon having lands and this too; you cannot at the same time be solicitous for your paltry slaves and yourself too. But if you wish for any one of the things that are not your own, what is your own is lost. This is the nature of the matter: Nothing is done except for a price. (4.10.18–19)

Epictetus cites faithfulness and self-respect as things which are one's own,[14] and we can see how flattering officials and groveling before them in order to be awarded a consulship would entail losing those very same qualities. 'If I admire my paltry body, I have given myself away as a slave; if I admire my paltry property, I have given myself away as a slave; for at once I show thereby to my own hurt what I can be caught with' (1.25.23–4). One subjects oneself to the exploitation and manipulation of others by valuing things which are under their control. Thus by admiring an external one in effect gives oneself away as a slave.

> For that which is not in your power to acquire or to keep is none of yours. Keep far away from it not merely your hands, but above all your desire; otherwise, you have delivered yourself

into slavery, you have bowed your neck to the burden, if you admire anything that is not your own, if you conceive a violent passion for anything that is in subjection to another and mortal. (4.1.77)

The desire for externals yokes one under the burden of pursuing something subject to the whims of another. One is then led around like a slave by this desire. Thus in desiring any external one is selling one's own self-mastery away: 'For you are the one that knows yourself, how much you are worth in your own eyes and at what price you sell yourself' (1.2.11; cf. 1.2.33).

Again it must be emphasized that Epictetus does not conceive of any compromise in which both externals and internals (virtues) can be sought and obtained. He holds that if one limits one's desires to a modest number of things, one stands a good chance of acquiring them, whereas if one tries to satisfy many desires one is doomed to fail to satisfy them: 'do not desire many things and you will obtain' (3.3.22). Because the nature of the possible objects of desire divides fundamentally into two quite disparate classes on Epictetus' view, one is faced with an equally rigid dichotomy of choices which does not allow one to split one's attention. 'You must be one person, either good or bad; you must labour to improve either your own governing principle or externals; you must work hard either on the inner man, or on things outside; that is, play the role of a philosopher, or else that of a layman' (3.15.13). Here Epictetus uses the traditional Stoic term *to hēgemonikon*, (governing principle), to refer to that which controls the 'internals' which are 'up to us.'

Thus five different reasons for confining the good to internals and not desiring externals can be found in Epictetus: (1) the unavoidable hindrance in the acquisition of externals, (2) the difficulty of managing externals, (3) the insecurity of the continued possession of externals, (4) the hostile mutual competition for externals, and (5) the sacrifice of moral worth for externals. For Epictetus these reasons are certainly more than enough to establish that reason dictates that one consider only the things which are truly one's own as goods worth desiring and attending to.

Consequently, for one to desire externals as if they were real goods and to pursue them with that attitude is without doubt contrary to reason. But Epictetus makes his case for this first principle of his Stoicism stronger still. He maintains that even if you can and do, somehow, successfully manage to acquire and retain many externals, you will continue to feel the need for more, because although you may have material wealth, fame, political power, etc., you will need what you do not have, namely, 'steadfastness, your mind in accord with nature, freedom from disturbance.'[15] These vital elements of happiness in the Epictetan conception simply cannot be gained from externals. He will argue that they derive only from the virtuous condition of the *prohairesis* (faculty of choice/volition). It is this which Epictetus takes to be the only real source of both good and evil, and therefore both the only subject of moral evaluation and the sole determining factor of a person's well-being. We shall see, moreover, that Epictetus indeed considers the *prohairesis* to be the true locus of the self.

B. *Prohairesis* as self

As we would expect, Epictetus certainly includes 'volition and all the acts of volition' (1.22.10) among the things up to us, but *prohairesis* is special because, as we shall soon see, the other things 'up to us' are contained by it. He states that 'the volition is naturally free and not subject to compulsion, while *everything* else is liable to interference and compulsion, subject to others and not our own' (2.15.1). He adds that one's own *prohairesis* is 'the only thing in which one can have confidence – in what is faithful, free from hindrance, cannot be taken away' (3.26.24). The *prohairesis* is by its nature free from hindrance and constraint because one is free to assent only to truth and nobody can force one to accept the false (1.17.21–2). This is supported elsewhere when he asserts that one's *sunkatathesis* (assent) cannot be hindered (4.1.69–72).

A brief statement of the role of assent in the orthodox Stoic theory of agency is in order here. As Inwood has observed,[16] assent is vital to the Stoic analysis of action because it is the locus of moral responsibility. Inwood uses 'presentations' to refer to *phantasiai*, and terms *lekta* the 'propositions' to which assent (*sunkatathesis*) is given or withheld.

> The power of reason gives man the ability to form *lekta* which spell out the significance of his presentations in clear linguistic form; thus unlike children and animals, whose presentations are confused and inarticulate, an adult has the ability to spell out the meaning of his presentations and so the ability to assent to them.[17]

Upon the dawn of reason at age 14 a human being's *phantasiai* become rational *phantasiai*, the *lekta* which interpret them become articulate, and the hormetic impulse which prior to adulthood immediately triggered behavior is now a necessary but not always a sufficient condition for initiating human action. The rational agent must assent to the *lekton* 'This cake is to be eaten now.' He is not unthinkingly, instinctively and as it were magnetically dragged into action merely by noticing the cake.

Epictetus staunchly maintains the traditional Stoic position that the actions of an adult are not and can never be motivated by irrational impulses that drag the agent into motion without his assent; rather, the adult agent acts as he does out of the fully conscious judgement that he should act that way. Our judgements (*dogmata*) are determined by our *prohairesis* and so they are completely within our power to choose. As will be seen immediately and in the next section, in Epictetus it is the *dogmata* (judgements) which basically function as the *lekta* do in the psychology of action of the early Stoa. It is the *prohairesis* which is the faculty which determines our *dogmata*, and it is in this determination that we possess absolute freedom and thereby assume total moral responsibility. 'What a human action is will determine what a man is accountable for, since on the Stoic theory rational action, assented action, human action, and responsible action emerge as coextensive terms.'[18] Inwood should specify 'adult human action' above. With this specification I largely concur with his claim. The technical aspects of the Stoic theory of action are not of great importance in the *Diatribae*. I find no evidence that Epictetus substantially diverges from the orthodox account of assent.

Because of the complete autonomy regarding things 'up to you,' 'in this sphere you have a volition free from hindrance, constraint, obstruction' (1.17. 23). Epictetus thinks that to decide, to choose, is to be free: 'If you will (*theleis*), you are free; if you will (*theleis*), you will not have to blame anyone, or complain against anyone' (1.17.28).

The upshot of this is that in the province of one's *prohairesis* one is invincible (3.6.5–7). He observes, in his typically colorful way, that the tyrant can chain your leg and cut off your head, but that your *prohairesis* can neither be chained nor cut off (1.18.17). 'Who, then, is the invincible man? He whom nothing that is outside the sphere of his volition can dismay' (1.18.21). Epictetus emphasizes this potential invincibility of the *prohairesis* by proclaiming: 'My leg you will fetter, but my volition not even Zeus himself has power to overcome' (1.1.23). The theological reason Epictetus gives for this is that god[19] would no longer be god, nor would he be caring for us as he ought if it were not the case that he had given us our *prohairesis* from that part of himself which he has made such that it cannot be hindered by him or anyone else (1.17.27). The conclusion Epictetus draws from this is that '... this control over the volition is my true business, and in it neither shall a tyrant hinder me against my will, nor the multitude the single individual, nor the stronger man the weaker; for this has been given by god to each man as something that cannot be hindered' (4.5.34). There is, however, an entirely secular, non-theological reason why one's *prohairesis* is (or, to be more exact, is potentially) invincible and free from all hindrance, namely, only it can overcome itself. 'For nothing outside the sphere of the volition can hamper or injure the volition; it alone can hamper or injure itself' (3.19.2), 'and nothing else can overcome volition, but it overcomes itself' (1.29.12).

'But,' says someone, 'if a person subjects me to the fear of death. he compels me.' 'No, it is not what you are subjected to that impels you, but the fact that you decide it is better for you to do something of the sort than to die. Once more, then, it is the decision of your own judgement which compelled you, that is, volition compelled volition ...' (1.17.25–6)

This is why the *prohairesis* is potentially, but not necessarily always, invincible. The individual's own *prohairesis* can have complete freedom as long as this same *prohairesis* does not hinder itself. 'But what is by its very nature capable of hindering volition? Nothing that lies outside its sphere, but only itself *when perverted*. For this reason volition becomes the only vice, or the only virtue.'[20] Thus only if it is corrupted can one's *prohairesis* interfere with and hinder its own activity. Yet as long as one's *prohairesis* is kept in a healthy state, one will be invincible:

> ... for if you wish to maintain freedom of volition in its *natural* condition, all security is yours, every facility yours, you have no trouble. For if you are willing to keep guard over those things which are under your direct authority and by nature free, and if you are satisfied with them, what else do you care about?[21]

At this point a short explanatory digression is appropriate. In his zeal to emphasize that for the rational person the sole area of concern lies in prohairetic matters, Epictetus occasionally overstates the extent to which one ought to restrict one's desire. For example he proclaims, 'freedom is not acquired by satisfying yourself with what you desire, but by destroying your desire' (4.1.175).

Now the complete elimination of desire would certainly seem to be humanly impossible, and although Epictetus does call for the student of Stoicism to overcome a great many basic human weaknesses, what Epictetus really meant to say here can be seen from the next two passages:

> Remember that it is not merely desire for office and wealth which makes men abject and subservient to others, but desire also for peace, and leisure, and travel, and scholarship. For it makes no difference what the external object be, the value you set upon it makes you subservient to another. (4.4.1)

Later on in this same chapter he finally clarifies exactly what he is enjoining us to do and why.

> And how shall I free myself? – Have you not heard over and over again that you ought to eradicate desire utterly, direct your aversion towards the things that lie within the sphere of the volition, and these things only, that you ought to give up everything, your body, your property, your reputation, your books, turmoil, office, freedom from office? For if once you swerve aside from this course, you are a slave, you are a subject, you have become liable to hindrance and to compulsion, you are entirely under the control of others. (4.4.33)

Clearly, then, Epictetus is using *epithumia* and *orexis* in the layman's sense of desire for externals. *This* is the kind of desire that must be utterly eliminated and replaced strictly with desire for and attention to prohairetic things. In fact, Epictetus describes the desire for prohairetic mastery in very positive terms elsewhere. He addresses the fully trained Stoic saying:

> ... you possess a harmonious and regulated desire for the things that are within the sphere of the volition, as being excellent, and as being within your reach; and you desire nothing outside the sphere of the volition, so as to give place to that other element of unreason, which pushes you along and is impetuous beyond all measure. (4.1.84)

In this latter passage Epictetus explicitly describes the desire for externals as irrational (*alogon*), and in the former passage he repeats that failure to restrict one's desire to prohairetic things subjects one to compulsion by enslaving oneself to the will of others. It should be sufficiently evident from these passages that the desire he urges us totally to destroy is the specific desire for externals, not desire in itself.

Now we may return to Epictetus' conclusion back at 2.23.19 that since only when it is perverted does it hinder itself, *prohairesis* becomes the only vice or the only virtue. He repeats this idea in a number of passages. 'Wherein lies the good? – In volition. – Wherein lies evil? – In volition. – Wherein lies that which is neither good nor evil? – In the things that lie outside the domain of volition' (2.16.1). This curt reminder sums up much of what Epictetus considers to be the heart of his teaching. Here again we can see that Epictetus is making his own personal formulation of a traditional view of the early Stoa. He is designating everything extra-prohairetic as neither good nor evil just as Zeno and Chrysippus designate everything other than virtue and vice as 'indifferent.'[22]

> If all of this is true and we are not silly nor merely playing a part when we say, 'Human good and evil lie in volition, and all other things are nothing to us,' why are we still distressed and afraid? Over the things that we seriously care for no one has authority; and the things over which other men have authority do not concern us. (1.25.1–2)

And again 'if you enquire of me what is the human good, I can give no other answer than that it is a kind of volition' (1.8.16).

At 1.18.8 Epictetus uses the superlative, stating that the greatest thing in each person is a right *prohairesis*. One reason for this is due to the use to which subordinate faculties are put:

> But if you ask me, 'What, then, is the highest of all things?' What shall I say? The faculty of eloquence? I cannot; but rather that of volition, when it becomes a right volition. For it is this which uses not only that faculty of eloquence but also all the other faculties both small and great; when this has been set right a man becomes good, when it has failed a man becomes bad; it is through this that we are unfortunate, and are fortunate, blame one another, and are pleased with one another; in a word, it is this which, when ignored, produces wretchedness, but when attended to produces happiness.[23]

Two points should be made here. First, the idea that the *prohairesis* 'uses' all the other faculties is very important because it is what determines whether the operation of a particular faculty[24] is used well or badly, properly or improperly, according to nature and therefore morally, or contrary to nature and hence immorally. We shall see this in more detail in the next chapter when we discuss the idea that although externals are morally neutral intrinsically, i.e. neither good nor bad, the use which we make of them is not morally neutral for Epictetus.

The second point to be noticed about this last passage is how the *prohairesis* is the key factor in the moral status of the individual. Epictetus says that if a person's *prohairesis* has been set right, then the person becomes good, while conversely if it has 'failed' then the person becomes bad. This is because the *prohairesis* not only controls[25] the senses, but as we will see in the next section, it is the faculty which tells the individual what to believe or disbelieve and how to act or not act (2.23.9–14). All we need stress here is that one's *eudaimonia* turns entirely on whether one closely attends to one's *prohairesis* or neglects it.

Epictetus is very consistent on this point: 'The essence of the good is a certain kind of volition, and that of the evil is a certain kind of volition' (1.29.1). As he suggests in 1.23.27–9, conflict and blame are eliminated once what is truly good and evil has been determined.

> But if the right kind of volition and that alone is good, and if the wrong kind of volition and that alone is bad, where is there any longer room for contention, where for reviling? About what? About the things that mean nothing to us? Against whom? Against the ignorant, against the unfortunate, against those who have been deceived in the most important values? (4.5.32)

Epictetus reasons that if the Stoic contains his concern within his own *prohairesis*, then he will be freed from squabbles and conflicts with others over externals. Since good and evil lie completely within one's own *prohairesis*, it is completely under the individual's control and within his power and his power alone to affect for good or ill his moral character. Consequently, his mental well-being also lies under his own control. Thus for Epictetus there is no such thing as moral luck since the moral status of each individual is totally self-determined.

> What are the things, then, to which I ought to pay attention? – First, these general principles, and you ought to have them at your command, and without them neither go to sleep, nor rise up, nor drink, nor eat, nor mingle with people; I mean the following: No one is master of another's volition; and: In its sphere alone are to be found one's good and evil. It follows, therefore, that no one has power either to procure me good, or to involve me in evil, but I myself alone have authority over myself in these matters. Accordingly, when these things are secure for me, what excuse have I for being disturbed about things external? (4.12.7–9)

Having located one's good and evil exclusively within one's own *prohairesis*, Epictetus infers that no ground remains for being disturbed by externals. This is because he holds that the only thing which causes a disturbance (i.e. a *pathos*) is a bad *prohairesis* (namely, one which makes incorrect *dogmata*), and no externals can in themselves make one's *prohairesis* bad.

The concept of *prohairesis* is central to Epictetus' ethics because he regards this faculty of choice, this decision-maker, this locus of moral agency and self-determiner, as the very essence of the person. As we have seen from the last passage, no one is master over another's *prohairesis*. Exercising total authority within it, each person has, as it were, absolute sovereignty within her prohairetic realm. This distinguishes it as the factor of agency of the individual, and consequently Epictetus even goes so far as to identify one's *prohairesis* with one's inner self.[26] Epictetus replies to the person who complains that his crockery has been broken by scolding: 'Are you a piece of crockery, then? No, but you are volition.'[27] Here he is observing that it is ridiculous to allow the loss of a material possession to be a cause of distress to the self since the destruction of the former need in no way injure the latter. Similarly, he also maintains that one ought not be overly occupied with the beauty of one's body, '[b]ecause *you* are not flesh, nor hair, but volition; if you get that beautiful, then you will be beautiful.'[28] The idea here is that genuine beauty is beauty of the self, and this is to be found in the good condition of one's *prohairesis*,[29] not in the appearance of one's body.[30]

Epictetus repeats this idea about the beautiful, saying

> ... that it arises in that part of you where you have your reason; seek it where you have your choices and your refusals, where you have your desires and your aversions. For this part is something of a special kind which you have within you but your paltry body is by nature only clay. (4.11.26–7)

It is *logos* which distinguishes human beings from children and non-human animals. So while bodies are common to all animals, the faculty of reason which governs choices and refusals, desires and aversions, is special to adult humans.

Epictetus elaborates on how the reasoning faculty (*hē dunamis hē logikē*) is special by observing that it is the only faculty which contemplates both itself and everything else, since it and it alone determines how to make use of sense-impressions (*phantasiai*) (1.1.4–6). It is just this power of judging how to use sense-impressions which exalts one's *logos* 'for as to reason you are not inferior to the gods, nor less than they; for the greatness of reason is not determined by length nor by height, but by judgements' (1.12.26).

I will suggest below that Epictetus reserves the word *prohairesis* for what I am disposed to call the self. This suggestion is at least partially supported by Voelke's emphasis on its active force:

> ... the term *prohairesis* underlines forcefully a feature that the terms *logos* or *hegemonikon* do not mark to the same degree. Indeed it has a strongly active sense and designates either an action, or the power or function that presides over the execution of that action. It is difficult to make precise to which extent the function is really distinct from the action for Epictetus. Anyway, it is in and through an abstraction that one can separate them both.[31]

That our true nature, our real self, lies in our cognitive powers is strongly implied when Epictetus urges the beautification of 'that which is our true nature – the reason, its judgements, its activities.'[32] We are now naturally led to examine the pivotal role 'judgements' (*dogmata*) play in Epictetus' ethics.

C. Judgements determine everything

Epictetus contrasts *dogmata* with all other possessions by pointing out that they can never be lost or taken away. He explains that exile is no cause of alarm because

> [w]herever I go it will be well with me, for here where I am it was well with me, not because of my location, but because of my judgements, and these I shall carry away with me; nor, indeed, can any man take these away from me, but they are the only things that are mine, and they cannot be taken away, and with the possession of them I am content, wherever I be and whatever I do. (4.7.14)

Now it is certainly no accident that one's judgements cannot be separated from oneself. The relationship between the two is so intimate on Epictetus' view that the former both stand decided witness to the moral character of the latter (the worth of the self being revealed by its judgements), and entirely determine the degree of happiness or misery of the latter. That is why the educated person is content with possessing only the right judgements. We shall now see how Epictetus arrives at these conclusions.

First we can begin by observing Epictetus' strong and consistently maintained Socratic conviction[33] that 'one person does not harm another, but that it is one's own actions which both harm and help him ...' (4.13.8). How it is that one can either harm or benefit oneself and that no one else can do this will be clarified below. But what does Epictetus consider to be the cause of a person's actions? He insists 'we ought not to look for the motive anywhere outside of ourselves, but that in all cases it is one and the same thing that is the cause of our doing a thing or of our not doing it ...' (1.11.28). The impetus of all our actions lies within us. We are not, in fact, caused (determined) to act or refrain from acting by any external threats or circumstances. 'And, in brief, it is neither death, nor exile, nor toil, nor any such thing that is the cause of our doing, or of our not doing, anything, but only our opinions and our judgements (*dogmata*)' (1.11.33). It is the judgement (*dogma*) made or decided upon by the agent which moves him to act as he does. No one is ever truly coerced by another, according to Epictetus' psychology of agency, because it is only one's body, possessions, and associates which are subject to physical force, but never the judgements of one's *prohairesis*. The tyrant may say to us:

> 'Yes, but I wish to control your judgements also.' And who has given you this authority? How can you have the power to overcome another's judgement? 'By bringing fear to bear,' he says, 'I shall overcome you.' You fail to realize that the judgement overcame itself, it was not overcome by something else. (1.29.11–12)

A judgement can only be overcome by another judgement. When faced with the threat of death one is never truly compelled by *that*, but if one is in fact compelled, 'once more, then, it is your own *dogma* which compelled you, that is, volition compelled volition' (1.17.26). Thus one's *prohairesis* overcomes itself (as in 3.19.2 and 1.29.11–12) by replacing one *dogma* with another, by supplanting one of its judgements with another.

Epictetus' conception of the *prohairesis* (as what I should like to call the self) is a deliberate invention designed to make room for moral accountability within the rigid material determinism of the Stoic universe. This innovation is Epictetus' attempt to salvage the freedom of the self, which is a *sine qua non* for voluntary agency and hence moral responsibility. Voelke observes that the verbs *thelein* and *boulesthai* are used quite frequently in the *Diatribae*, but scarcely at all in the earlier Stoics.[34] If Zeus had not given humans a part of his divine self (the *prohairesis*), which cannot be constrained or controlled by anything external to it, then human choices, decisions, and actions would be determined by Zeus' will either via vertical causality, or horizontally via the corporeal, organic constitution of things, or both.

Epictetus deduces from this that our judgements express and, as it were, stand witness to the kind of person we are. The moral character of a person is decisively revealed by that person's judgements. In other words, the character of the self is visibly disclosed by its judgements: 'For a human being is not something like a stone or a stick of wood to be pointed out with a finger, but when one shows his judgements, then one shows him as a human being' (3. 2.12). Thus Epictetus holds that one is measured by one's judgements – to understand someone's judgements (*dogmata*) is to understand her inner self.

> The person who meets a human being as a human being is one who learns to understand the other's judgements, and in his turn exhibits his own. Learn to know my judgements; show me your own, and then say you have met me. Let us put one another to the test; if I cherish any evil judgement, take it away; if you cherish one, bring it forward. That is what it means to meet a philosopher. (3.9.12–13)

Philosophers who are genuine lovers of wisdom probe, scrutinize, and critically assess the fundamental evaluative judgements of selves. They join together to perform meticulous and mutual self-examination in order to understand who they are, what they believe, value, and respect, and why.

Epictetus uses a clever analogy to illustrate the relation between a person's judgements and their moral character. Just as we accept coins as valid legal tender only if the imprints they bear mark them as such. so should we inspect a person's judgements in order to assess the quality of that person's character before accepting him:

> What imprint do his judgements bear? 'He is gentle, generous, patient, affectionate.' Give him to me. I accept him. I make this man a citizen, I accept him as a neighbour and a fellow-

voyager. Only see that he does not have the imprint of Nero. Is he choleric, furious, querulous? 'If he feels like it, he punches the heads of the people he meets.' Why, then, did you call him a human being? For surely everything is not judged by its outward appearance only, is it? (4.5.17–19)

Similarly, he reasons, just as the external outline of an object which looks like an apple does not provide sufficient ground for calling it an apple unless it also smells and tastes like one, 'neither are the nose and the eyes sufficient to prove that one is a human being, but you must see whether one has the judgements that belong to a human being' (4.5.20).

There are two senses at work in 'being human.' Nero is human in the sense that he operates according to the natural constitution of a member of *Homo sapiens sapiens.* There is also a certain minimal set of normatively decent *dogmata* which, if one fails to have them, then one does not deserve to be counted a human, i.e. a humane being, at all. In this sense Nero fails to qualify as human since some of his *dogmata* degrade and dehumanize him. Epictetus refuses to dignify someone who lacks sufficiently virtuous judgements with the designation 'human.' He prefers to regard such a pugnacious individual as 'some wild beast.'[35]

The moral worth of an action turns on the *dogma* made by the agent in so acting. If the judgement upon which the agent acts is a good one, then that action is itself good. However, if the judgement motivating the action is evil, then, according to Epictetus, the action is necessarily evil. For I would not have you either praise or blame a man for things that may be either good or bad, but only for judgements. Because these are each man's own possessions, which make his actions either base or noble' (4.4.44). Epictetus says in the context of this remark that a person is only truly industrious if the end for which he vigorously strives is a virtuous one (in this case, having his *hēgemonikon* in accord with nature). This is a very significant point. Epictetus holds that the moral goodness or evil of an action is entirely determined by the judgement (*dogma*) from which the agent acts, because it is this judgement which truly belongs to the agent. Evidently, then, any positive or negative consequences of an action are, for the purposes of evaluating the moral goodness of that action (and thus the moral status of the agent who performs it), irrelevant. Clearly this must be because any results or consequences of a particular action are not strictly under the control of the agent and so are not the agent's 'own possessions.' For this reason Epictetus considers them outside the realm of moral evaluation.

Epictetus' position, consequently, is that the judgement which leads the agent to act is the sole factor to consider in the moral evaluation of an agent's action. Until one can ascertain what that motivating judgement is, one is in no position to assess the action, since the action, separated from its motivating judgement, is neither good nor bad,

> ... only the act which proceeds from correct judgements is well done, and that which proceeds from bad judgements is badly done. Yet until you learn the judgement from which a man performs each separate act, neither praise nor blame it. But a judgement is not readily determined by externals. (4.8.3)

By this last warning Epictetus means that one cannot simply read the agent's judgement off his sleeve, as it were. The *dogma* cannot be observed externally because it lies within the agent himself. Thus one would need to question the agent in order to elicit the motivating judgement from him. Then the dogma issued by his *prohairesis* could be identified.

One's judgements, however, also determine one's own well-being. Whether or not something harms one depends on what the individual judges to be important. Now, we see how only the individual is in a position to help or harm himself. Epictetus insists that it is only one's judgements that can provide safety and security for oneself. Just as a city whose walls are safe and whose citizens have sufficient food and supplies cannot be captured by external besiegers, nothing but judgements make similarly secure the soul of a human being (4.5.25–6). Epictetus goes on to explain that no wall is as strong and no body as invincible, no possession as secure against theft and no reputation as unassailable as one's own judgements (4.5.26). All these things are perishable and easy to capture, but our judgements are the one means of safety available to us. Consequently, Epictetus infers that given this state of affairs we would be silly not to be willing to give up the many perishable and unfree things in order to devote ourselves to those things which are naturally free, i.e. our *dogmata*. He then urges us to remember that 'no one either hurts or helps another, but ... it is his judgement about each of these things which is the thing that hurts him, that overturns him' (4.5.28). Real harm and real help, Epictetus contends, come only from one's own judgements about things, so one can only affect *oneself* for better or worse, one cannot truly harm or be harmed, help or be helped by another. There is a parallel of considerable importance between Epictetus' *dogma* and Kant's maxim of the will, but an adequate discussion of this would certainly merit its own separate treatment.

We must bear in mind that for Epictetus true harm and help do not pertain to the body or anything else external to the *prohairesis*, but only to the true self, the *prohairesis* itself. He is definitely not implying here that one cannot aid a person who is in a difficult or dangerous situation. The external circumstances of such a situation certainly can be affected by the efforts of the person rendering help.[36] Rather, Epictetus is simply asserting that it is the individual's own judgement about that situation which harms or helps his true self – neither the external circumstances, nor the acts or omissions of another, can affect that.

The consequence of all this is that when we feel constrained or hampered, Epictetus maintains that this is not the result of any external state of affairs, but rather something we bring upon ourselves. 'For in general remember this – that we crowd *ourselves*, we make close quarters for *ourselves*, that is to say, the decisions of our will (*ta dogmata*) crowd us and make us close quarters.'[37] It is our freely chosen judgements which make us feel this way. We have in fact decided to feel this way.

Moreover, our judgements are, unsurprisingly, the cause of our more severe disquietude. 'What, then, are the things that weigh upon us and drive us out of our senses? Why, what else but our judgements?' (2.16.24). One may object that this insistence on one's intellectual appraisals of events as the real source of psychic suffering simply fails to recognize the 'real tragedies' of life.[38] Yet Epictetus is not at all ignoring the tragic aspect of life. Rather, this is precisely what he diagnoses. 'For what are tragedies but the portrayals in tragic verse of the sufferings of people who have admired things external?' (1.4.26). The people he cites here are Priam and Oedipus. Elsewhere mentioning Agamemnon, Achilles, the *Atreus* of Euripides, the *Oedipus* of Sophocles, the Phoenix and the *Hippolytus*, Epictetus repeats this idea that tragedy has no other source than inattentively following every haphazard sense-impression (1.28.31–3). He tries to debunk the notion that 'real' tragedy arises despite our best efforts to avoid it. 'Behold how tragedy arises, when everyday events befall fools!' (2.16.31). A critic like Nussbaum may object that Stoics trivialize the force of tragic episodes. I think that the Stoics want to insist on the invulnerability of the sage's goodness not *despite* the occurrence of 'tragedies,' but rather *because* of the occurrence of events which are commonly called tragedies. The Stoics refuse to think of goodness as fragile and contingent.

In any case, Epictetus is quite consistent in holding that '[i]t is not possible that that which is by nature free should be disturbed or thwarted by anything but itself. But it is his judgements that disturb him' (1.19.7–8). Only the self, through its own judgements, can be the cause of its own perturbation. The individual creates sorrow for himself by means of his judgement, and his grief will remain as long as he retains it (2.16.40). Again at 3.19.3 Epictetus repeats 'that nothing but judgement is responsible for the disturbance of our peace of mind and our inconstancy ...' He is relentlessly consistent in maintaining that it is one's own judgements which are invariably the cause of one's mental disturbance, grief, sorrow, uneasiness, and inconstancy.

Of course one's judgements certainly need not necessarily be the cause of all this unhappiness. Nevertheless, it is the case that misery will inevitably accompany certain judgements.

> For where there are disturbances, and griefs, and fears, and ineffectual desires, and unsuccessful avoidances, and envies,

and jealousies – where is there in the midst of all this a place for
happiness to enter? But wherever worthless judgements (*sapra
dogmata*) are held, there all these passions must necessarily exist.
(3.22.61)

It is *sapra dogmata,* 'rotten opinions,' which necessitate all these
elements of misery. These rotten opinions are the one which
debase the person and disrupt mental harmony. The following
passage is worth quoting at length because in it Epictetus explains
clearly how many evils result from the single judgement which
places the good outside one's *prohairesis.*

> Nay, do not make the same enquiry that most men do, asking
> whether two men are of the same parents, or were brought up
> together, or had the same school attendant, but this, and this
> only: Where do they put their interest – outside themselves, or
> in their volition? If outside, call them not friends, any more than
> you would call them faithful, steadfast, courageous, or free; nay,
> call them not even human beings, if you are wise. For it is no
> judgement of human sort which makes them bite (that is revile)
> one another, and take to the desert (that is, to the market-place)
> as wild beasts take to the mountains, and in courts of law act
> the part of brigands; nor is it a judgement of human sort which
> makes them profligates and adulterers and corrupters; nor is it
> any such thing which makes men guilty of any of the many other
> crimes which they commit against one another; it is because
> of one single judgement, and this alone – because they put
> themselves and what belongs to themselves in the category of
> things which lie outside the sphere of volition. (2.22.26–8)

So the subhuman *dogma* that what matters to the person lies outside
her *prohairesis* is what brings upon her all these vices. This *dogma* by
itself serves to determine the moral deficiency of the person who
holds it.

But if you hear these people assert that in all sincerity they believe
the good to be where volition lies, and where there is the right

use of impressions, then you need no longer trouble yourself as to whether they are son and father, or brothers, or have been schoolmates a long time and are comrades; but though this is the only knowledge you have concerning them, you may confidently declare them 'friends,' just as you may declare them 'faithful' and 'upright.' For where else is friendship to be found than where there is fidelity, respect, a devotion to things honourable and to nothing else? (2.22.29–30)

Thus Epictetus believes that upholding the *dogma* that the good lies within one's *prohairesis* is by itself a sufficient guarantee that one possesses the virtues upon which true friendship is based. If this judgement is sincerely held, then this constitutes sufficient evidence for the moral excellence of the person who holds it, because it indicates he values moral choice and virtuous intention and will act accordingly.

Thus the evil, worthless judgements that are the cause of all ills are just those judgements which put value on externals.

These, then, are the vicious judgements which we ought to eradicate; this is the subject upon which we ought to concentrate our efforts. Why, what is weeping and sighing? A judgement. What is misfortune? A judgement. What are strife, disagreement, fault-finding, accusing, impiety, foolishness? They are all judgements, and that, too, judgements about things that lie outside the province of volition, assumed to be good or evil. Let someone but transfer his judgements to matters that lie within the province of the volition, and I guarantee that he will be steadfast, whatever be the state of things about him. (3.3.18–19; cf. also 3.5.4)

Even non-verbal responses like weeping and sighing Epictetus counts as *dogmata* since they are displays of negative assessments of things external to one's *prohairesis*. It is just this assumption that any external is good or bad which Epictetus wants to reject as false. If one can eliminate all such judgements and turn her concern and her evaluations of good and evil to matters that lie exclusively within her faculty of choice, the use of impressions, and what is

up to her, i.e. her moral intention and decisions, then her steadfastness will be guaranteed regardless of the state of affairs that
surround her.

Consequently, Epictetus maintains that judgements are all-
important: 'If you have sound judgements, you will fare well; if
unsound judgements, ill; since in every case the way one fares is
determined by one's judgement' (3.9.2). Thus he believes that
pantōn aitia ta dogmata, 'judgements determine everything' or
'judgements are responsible for everything' (3.9.4).[39]

Now external things are not, in fact, going to be irrelevant
when it comes to the operation of the *prohairesis* and the judgements which it issues because the judgements are most often about
externals. Having stated that the essence of the good is one kind
of *prohairesis*, while that of the evil is another kind of *prohairesis*
(1.29.1), Epictetus asks:

> What, then, are the external things? They are the materials for
> the volition, in dealing with (*anastrephesthai*) which it will find its
> own proper good or evil. How will it find the good? If it does not
> admire the materials. For the judgements about the materials, if
> they be correct, make the volition good, but if they be crooked
> and awry, they make it evil. (1.29.2–3)

This further clarifies the interrelation of *prohairesis* and *dogmata*.
The *prohairesis* is the faculty which formulates *dogmata*. The *dogmata*,
if they are virtuous in content, mark the *prohairesis* as good, while
conversely if they are vicious they are symptomatic of a bad,
unhealthy prohairesis. In this next passage Epictetus appears to
refer to the same faculty although he uses '*psychē*.'

> And the functions of a soul are the exercise of choice, of
> refusal, of desire, of aversion, of preparation, of purpose, and of
> assent. What, then, can that be which makes the soul dirty and
> unclean in these functions? Nothing but its erroneous decisions
> (*krimata*). It follows, therefore, that impurity of a soul consists
> of bad judgements (*dogmata ponēra*), and purification consists in
> creating within it the proper kind of judgements; and a pure soul

is the one which has the proper kind of judgements, for this is the only soul which is secure against confusion and pollution in its own functions. (4.11.6–8)

The soul (*psychē*), makes itself pure or corrupt by means of what its *prohairesis* chooses, refuses, desires, avoids, or in other words, how it decides to use the external impressions it receives by way of the judgements it makes about them.

But what are the proper kind of judgements which the pure soul (the one which has the right kind of volition) has? First, it is to remember what is 'up to us' and what is not 'up to us.' Epictetus proclaims that Odysseus put his trust '[n]ot in reputation, or money, or office, but in his own might, that means, his judgements about the things which are under our control, and those which are not under our control. For these are the only things that make people free, that make them unhampered ...' (3.26.34–5). To keep in mind what is 'up to me' and what is not 'up to me' and to judge these things accordingly is what frees the individual from the inevitable hindrances resulting from judging something one's own that is *not* one's own. This is why Epictetus says that 'to be getting an education means this: To be learning what is your own, and what is not your own.'[40] This is exactly the education which Stoicism is meant to provide. If one succeeds in gaining this education, one's serenity will thereby be ensured.

This perpetual freedom from disturbance ensues, however, only if one also makes the judgement that her good and evil lie exclusively within those things 'up to her' which are truly 'her own.' So the second kind of judgement necessary for a healthy, purified *prohairesis* is that moral value is to be found always and only within one's own *prohairesis*. Epictetus describes this as if it were an immutable equation akin to a divine law: 'Whoever shall regard as good anything but the things that fall within the scope of his volition, let him envy, yearn, flatter, feel disturbed; whoever shall regard anything else as evil, let him sorrow, grieve, lament, be unhappy. (3.11.2). One's happiness or misery turns completely upon this single, inescapable law of our human condition. But despite the fact that Epictetus likens this equation to a divine law, we shall now see that the validity of the primary choice which this state of affairs demands relies on no theological or cosmological commitments.

D. The status of the location of the good

Epictetus is so keenly aware of the benefits of Stoic education that he makes the following revealing remark:

> If indeed one had to be deceived into learning that among things external and independent of our free choice (*aprohaireton*) none concerns us, I, for my part, should consent to a deception which would result in my living thereafter serenely and without turmoil; but as for you, you will yourselves see to your own preference. (1.4.27)

What Epictetus recognizes in this remarkably insightful passage is that genuine belief in the judgement that all things external to one's *prohairesis* are of no concern is sufficient by itself for producing a serene and unperturbed way of life. Whatever trivialities the Stoic philosopher may give up in adhering to this doctrine, she secures by means of it *apatheia*, *eleutheria*, and *ataraxia* (3.15.12; *Ench.* 29.7). But does this mean that Epictetus values *ataraxia* more than *eudaimonia?* 'What, then, is the fruit of these doctrines? Precisely that which must needs be both the fairest and the most becoming for those who are being truly educated – tranquillity, fearlessness,[41] freedom' (2.1.21). All those who have truly learned the doctrines of Stoicism will necessarily receive all these benefits. This is so simply in virtue of the state of mind this fundamental Stoic *dogma* brings about. This is why, according to Epictetus, the doctrine of the (Stoic) philosophers proclaims: 'Folks (*anthrōpoi*), if you heed me, wherever you may be, whatever you may be doing, you will feel no pain, no anger, no compulsion, no hindrance, but you will pass your lives in tranquillity and in freedom from every disturbance' (3.13.11). Again, all these benefits are gained simply by virtue of accepting the doctrine that extra-prohairetic matters are of no (moral) concern. Clearly, this is the reason why Epictetus admits he would consent to being deceived into 'learning,' that is to say choosing to believe, this doctrine at 1.4.27.[42]

In what, precisely, does this deception consist? In discussing what he calls this 'Cynic-Stoic idea that things external and beyond our control are nothing to us,' Jason Xenakis holds the view that 'No doubt, what is allowed to be illusory is not the Cynic-Stoic idea; rather, the way it is presented, in life or art. Still, the fact remains that as far as Epictetus is concerned, truth may be sacrificed to happiness or worrylessness.'[43] Now it is incontestable that Epictetus fervently believes that the judgement that externals are of no concern is true. However, Xenakis' second remark reveals an aspect of this judgement which carries a profound implication. Since belief in this judgement by itself suffices to secure for the believer the many happy benefits listed above, the truth of the judgement seems to follow inevitably. In other words, the Stoic who sincerely holds the judgement that externals are of no moral concern will necessarily receive the benefits of psychic tranquillity and freedom from worry as the 'fruit' of this doctrine (2.1.21). Xenakis thinks that the way this doctrine is presented (whether in the form of tragedies or whatever) is what Epictetus allows to be illusory. But I am more inclined to think that 'being deceived' into believing the Stoic line on externals is purely rhetorical, not epistemic. Epictetus would believe that externals are of no moral concern even if, *per impossibile*, it were false. But the fact that the belief works guarantees that the belief (*dogma*) is true.

Now one may object that when the Stoic judges externals to be of no concern he is simply indulging in self-deception when, having met with failure in getting what he truly does desire, he tells himself he never really desired those externals in the first place. I do not think this Sour Grapes objection can hold against the staunch, *bona fide* Stoic, however. If she genuinely believes in the judgement, then she will in fact not consider them as real goods at all. She won't just be trying to fool herself. As long as her belief in the intrinsic moral neutrality of externals stands firm, there seem to me no grounds for claiming that she is simply rationalizing away the real disappointment she 'must experience' at their loss, and that she is deceiving herself in denying that she values them as eudaimonic goods when, in fact, she does just that. The objection that she must consider externals as more than 'worthwhile' (*axia*) but full-blown intrinsic 'goods' (*agatha*) which necessarily affect her *eudaimonia* because it is simply humanly impossible not to, will be addressed in Chapter 4. In any case, Epictetus thinks Stoicism 'demonstrates the truth about happiness' (1.4.32).

The strength of Epictetus' conviction in the judgement that externals are of no (moral) concern which leads Xenakis to describe his consent to the life-enhancing 'deception' of 1.4.27 as a readiness to ignore truth or sacrifice truth for the sake of happiness or worrylessness[44] has led others to write: 'Epictetus' attitude towards his doctrine is to be called a religious attitude rather than a philosophical one. There is no reserve in his accepting the Stoic truth. On the contrary: one feels a Newmanian certitude in him.'[45] This assessment is misleading. I contend that it overlooks the genuinely philosophical reasoning Epictetus employs in arguing for his doctrines and this judgement of where the good lies in particular. As I have shown in section A above, after having divided all things into those which are 'up to us' and those which are 'not up to us,' Epictetus gives five separate reasons for choosing to place the good solely in the former group. The psychological principle underlying these arguments which Epictetus assumes is self-evident is that we are happy when we obtain what we desire and avoid what we dislike, and are unhappy when our desires go unfulfilled and we encounter what we would avoid. Since this principle is what calls for the judgement to value as 'goods' unconditionally only things under our control, it is clear that no assumptions about the nature or existence of God, the providence of worldly events, or any other religious or theological speculations are necessary.

> For even if Epictetus's conception (of *prohairesis*) does have some distinctly theological overtones, his basic notion of achieving moral invulnerability by restricting our concerns to what is in our power is essentially an ideal of rational autonomy that is man-centered rather than God-centered.[46]

Following Kahn on this point, I suggest that Epictetus presents decidedly philosophical support for the judgement which locates the good exclusively within the *prohairesis*. This centerpiece of his ethical system and the stronger arguments which he marshals for it rest on entirely secular grounds.

Additional evidence that Epictetus' attitude toward his ethical doctrine lacks religious dogmatism is found when we notice that he sees the determination of the value of internals vs. externals as a fundamental choice each individual makes on her own. This is evident from his remarks at the end of 1.4.27: 'I for *my* part, should consent to a deception which would result in my living thereafter serenely and without turmoil; but as for you, you will yourselves see to your own preference.'[47] This attitude strikes me as devoid of any religious zealotry, since Epictetus is not preaching that Stoicism be embraced universally, but rather that each individual must make up her own mind after having weighed the consequences of the choice.

Finally, that Epictetus sees the fundamental ethical judgement of his Stoicism as a product of philosophical rigor rather than religious faith can be seen from his remarks at the beginning of 4.7. He observes that it is possible 'due to some madness or despair'[48] that one care not at all about having or not having property, wife, or children.

> Therefore, if madness can produce this attitude of mind toward the things which have just been mentioned, and also habit, as with the Galilaeans, cannot reason and demonstration teach one that god has made all things in the universe, and the whole universe itself, to be free from hindrance, and to contain its end in itself, and the parts of it to serve the needs of the whole? ... the rational animal possesses faculties that enable him to consider all these things, both that he is a part of them, and what kind of part of them he is, and that it is well for the parts to yield to the whole. (4.7.6)

(Oldfather notes that by 'Galilaeans' Epictetus is referring to the Christians.[49]) In this lengthy but illustrative passage Epictetus explicitly pronounces his ethical principles a product of rational argument *as distinguished from* that of despair, madness, or the 'habit' of those of the Christian faith. But could it be that since madness and reasoned argument are two different means of arriving at the very same judgement (i.e. that people and things external to one's *prohairesis* have no intrinsic moral worth) that this betokens a skewed pathology of the judgement itself? I will wrestle with this potentially damning criticism in Chapter 4.

In any case, not only does Epictetus consider his ethical doctrines as conclusions arrived at via philosophical argument, but as others have observed, whereas Aristotle held that ethics is not a fully demonstrative science since it must resort to probabilities and approximations, '[f]or Epictetus the whole of ethics, and the rest of philosophy as well, is entirely demonstrative. The philosopher has no use for mere probabilities in any field.'[50] Sherman's remarks on Stoicism, I believe, apply quite well to Epictetus on this matter.

> The Stoic faith is philosophic faith – a faith in reason – not a 'religion' in the usual sense of that word. Surely the faith of Stoicism hinges in part, at least, on the insistence that men could and should conduct their affairs as men inclined at all times to virtue. Quite literally, man is the master of his destiny and captain of his soul. This faith is religious, perhaps, if by religion one means not a belief in things unseen (as the belief in God is a faith), but a *passion*.[51]

As we have seen, Epictetus maintains that happiness is entirely up to the individual; it is a matter of self-determination. The judgements each person makes about what is good and what is bad by themselves determine her happiness or misery. If the individual constantly bears in mind what things are her own and thus completely under her control and what things are not, her reason will lead her to make the proper judgements about both that result in freedom from hindrance, disappointment, disturbance, frustration, anxiety, fear, greed, envy, blame, guilt and regret.

Notes

1. This translates *ep emoi*. Epictetus more often speaks of what is *eph hēmin*, 'up to us.'
2. *Ench.* 1.1: *tōn ontōn ta men estin eph hēmin, ta de ouk eph hēmin.*
3. *Ench.* 1.1: *kai eni logōi hosa hēmetera erga.*
4. Oldfather translates *phantasia* 'external impression,' yet in many cases *phantasia* seems rather to be a conceptual construct *within* the mind, of a physical object external to the mind. Thus it is like a mental image or perceived appearance. See Brennan (2005: 51–61).
5. *orthē chrēsis phantasiōn* 2.19.32 and 1.12.34. Also cf. 3.24.69 and 1.1.7.
6. De Lacy writes: 'The use (*chrēsis*) of appearances does not refer to any overt act of ours in manipulating external objects but rather to the way we receive appearances, test their validity, and relate to them our desires and impulses' (De Lacy, 1943: 114).
7. Oldfather's translation of 1.22.10. I generally follow the translations of Oldfather (1925/28), though sometimes I modify them.
8. Strictly speaking, pain, pleasure and *phantasiai* are internal to the mind. The proper use of externals are of course of concern to us, yet pleasure and pain, though in a sense 'internal,' are not of concern because they are morally unimportant. See the discussion of the Stoic's attitude toward bodily pleasure and pain below.
9. What Epictetus understands by this is a desire which counts its object as a *good*. The idea here is that we ought only be moved to something taken to be a good if it is a good, i.e. a thing which is 'our own.'
10. 4.10.6; cf. 4.4.15.
11. The Stoic sage has perfected her understanding so that how she receives the appearance of the cake, how she pictures it in her mind, is predisposed to her fully rational judgements. For an account of the sage see Chapter 4, section A.
12. Cf. Holbrook Jackson: 'The possession of a great many things,

even the best of things, tends to blind one to the real value of anything.'

13. See the discussion of Trump in Chapter 4.

14. 1.25.4: *to piston son, to aidēmon son*; cf. 1.28.21 where Epictetus says that if neither a man's *aidēmon* nor his *piston* (nor his *suneton*) are destroyed, then the man himself is also preserved. On *aidōs* see Kamtekar (1998).

15. Oldfather's translation of 3.9.17: *tou eustathein, tou kata phusin echein tēn dianoian, tou mē tarattesthai.*

16. Inwood (1985: 72).

17. *Ibid.* 74.

18. *Ibid.* 99.

19. In translating '*theos*' in passages like this one, Oldfather capitalizes it into 'God' even though the Greek itself is not capitalized. Epictetus' conception of Zeus allows him to use anthropomorphic, personal language in encouraging himself and his students to 'follow god's will.' Yet Epictetus is a Stoic, not a Christian. Stoic physics would seem to entail an immanent conception of the divine rather than a transcendent one. As in other matters, Epictetus is not terribly worried about technical consistency on non-practical affairs. The core of his ethical system can stand, as I will argue, even without a personal, transcendent god. See the splendid discussion in Long (2002: 142–72).

20. Emphasis mine; Oldfather's translation of 2.23.19.

21. Emphasis mine; Oldfather's translation of 2.2.2–3.

22. Since Zeno and Chrysippus apparently never speak of *prohairesis*, perhaps it roughly corresponds to their usage of *logos*.

23. Oldfather's emphasis in his translation of 1.23.27–9.

24. 'The supremacy of the *prohairesis* does not therefore introduce a duality between this power and the functions which it rules. On this point Epictetus is clearly opposed to Marcus Aurelius, who subordinates all the psychic functions to a transcendent instance, the mind or *nous*' (Voelke, 1973: 153). This is Bernard Reginster's translation of: 'La suprématie de la prohairésis n'introduit donc pas de dualite entre ce pouvoir et les fonctions qu'il régit. Sur ce point Epictète s'oppose

nettement à Marc-Aurèle, qui subordonne toutes les fonctions psychiques à une instance transcendante, l'esprit ou nous.'

25. In passages like 2.23.27–9 the *prohairesis* seems to function as the *hēgemonikon* does in early Stoicism in so far as it governs or regulates the use of the senses. Once again Epictetus does not seem concerned with punctilious consistency in the usage of his technical terms in these informal conferences.

26. Dragona-Monachou (1978–79: 277 and 299) says that the concept of *prohairesis* in Epictetus represents the entire ethical, intellectual entity of man, and that Epictetan *prohairesis* is the real, genuine man, his beliefs, convictions, and principles. See also Dobbin (1991). Graver (2003) traces likely Stoic antecedents of Epictetus' use of *prohairesis*.

27. Oldfather's emphasis in his translation of 4.5.12.

28. Oldfather's emphasis in his translation of 3.1.40.

29. Hijmans, commenting on 3.1.40, claims that this *prohairesis* 'is the principle of man's individuality. One must, however, be very careful not to interpret it as man's personality because it essentially lacks the aspect of individual characteristics as distinct and different from other people's characteristics' (Hijmans, 1959: 26). His point seems reasonable if by 'personality' he understands an individual's idiosyncratic traits and dispositions of character. Yet I am inclined to term *prohairesis* 'self' in this context because often Epictetus practically reifies it. It seems to function as that entity within a person which determines all her choices and actions. This is why I am tempted to conceive of it as the self: it embodies the individual's moral agency and thereby lies at the seat of one's personhood.

30. Cf. 3.13.17 where Epictetus says that someone can murder your *body*, but not *you*.

31. Bernard Reginster's translation of: 'Pourtant le terme prohairésis souligne avec force un aspect que les termes logos ou hégemonikon ne marquent pas au même degré. Il revêt en effet un sens fortement actif et désigne soit un acte, soit le pouvoir ou la fonction présidant à l'exécution de cet acte. Il est difficile de préciser jusqu'à quel point la fonction est vraiment distincte de l'acte pour Epictète. En tout état de

cause, c'est dans et par l'acte qu'elle se manifeste, et seule une abstraction peut l'en détacher' (Voelke, 1973: 154–5).

32. Oldfather's translation of 4.11.33: *ekeino ho pephukamen, ton logon, ta dogmata, tas energeias.* Cf. also 3.1.25–6.

33. Cf. G. M. A. Grube's translation of *Apology* 30cd: 'Neither Meletus nor Anytus can harm me in any way; he could not harm me, for I do not think it is permitted that a better man be harmed by a worse,' and 41cd: 'a good man cannot be harmed either in life or in death.'

34. Voelke (1973: 131–2).

35. Oldfather's translation of *ti pote agrion thērion* at 4.5.21.

36. The crucial question of *why* one would want to assist others will be addressed in Chapter 3.

37. My emphasis in Oldfather's translation of 1.25.28.

38. See Nussbaum (1986).

39. And reiterated by Voelke (1973: 133–4).

40. Oldfather's emphasis in his translation from 4.5.7 of *to paideuesthai tout' estin, manthanein ta idia kai ta allotria.*

41. Cf. 4.7.1–5 for how fearlessness is instilled by Stoic doctrines.

42. Of course Bonhöffer rightly remarks that this readiness to submit to deception is only to be understood hypothetically since it is exactly in achieving virtue and truth that Epictetus believes inner happiness is obtained. Bonhöffer writes that Epictetus' principle of eudaimonism entails that 'nothing else can be true, than what makes the person happy' Stephens, (1996a: 18).

43. Xenakis (1968: 97); emphasis his.

44. *Ibid.*, 96–7.

45. Hijmans (1959: 12).

46. Kahn (1988: 258).

47. My emphasis in Oldfather's translation of 1.4.27.

48. Oldfather's translation of *hypo tinos manias kai aponoias* in 4.7.5.

49. Oldfather (1928: 362). Bonforte writes that 'While Epictetus lived at a slightly later period than Jesus, it appears fairly certain that Epictetus never came into contact with any of the Christian teachers or with the philosophy that they taught'

(Bonforte, 1955: x). For a detailed account of the relation between Jesus' teachings and those of our philosopher, see Bonhöffer (1911).

50. De Lacy (1943: 118).
51. Sherman (1967: 34–5); emphasis his. Since 'passion' is one translation of *pathos*, the irony here is striking. Could it be that the Stoic is so determined to eliminate *pathē* from her soul that her unswerving determination transforms itself into a monomania, a full-blooded *pathos*?

Chapter 2

How must I view the use of externals?

As we saw in Chapter 1, Epictetus regards all things 'not up to me' as indifferent *per se*. Epictetus must maintain that one's material possessions, reputation, friends, family, bodily health, and even one's own life are all in themselves morally neutral since they are not unconditionally good (*agathon*), but merely conditionally, provisionally, and instrumentally worthwhile (*axia*).[1] This is because they lie outside my control, that is, outside my volition, that is, my *prohairesis* (which he sometimes seems to equate with the self), within which all true good and evil reside, specifically, in the judgements (*dogmata*) which determine all my valuations of things and motivate all my actions. The Stoic wants and cares about many things that do not pertain directly to her good (*agathon*). In desiring *ta kala* ('nice' or 'fine' things), however, the Stoic does not desire them because they are 'good' for her. She may and often does want the pleasure of her meal, for example – i.e. how it will please her palate. The nutritional benefits, and the health which they promote, on the other hand, are separate goods. Thus there are different impulses directed toward objects with different types of positive value.[2] Unconditional value, according to Epictetus, is located exclusively within the prohairetic sphere and all other value obtains in relation, either directly or indirectly, to it.

In this respect Epictetus is not a heretic, but rather a popularizer of early Stoic doctrines. This is evident from the following passage:

Therefore Chrysippus well says, 'As long as the consequences are not clear to me, I cleave ever to what is better adapted to secure those things that are in accordance with nature; for god himself has created me with the faculty of selecting things (*eklektikon*). But if I really knew that it was ordained for me to be ill at this present moment, I would be impelled toward illness; for the foot also, if it had a mind, would be impelled toward being covered with mud.' (2.6.9–10)

This[3] clearly indicates that Epictetus accepts and simply takes for granted the orthodox theory of non-moral value 'according to nature' in the broad sense). My interpretation does not conflict with Bonhöffer, though it does contradict Le Hir[4] and also possibly Pohlenz.[5]

Given this account one is naturally led to ask: 'What, then, are the external things? They are materials (*hulai*) for volition, in dealing with which it will find its own proper good or evil. How will it find the good? If it does not admire the materials' (1.29.2–3). This explanation does not get us very far, however. If 'dealing with' external things in the proper way consists merely in not admiring them, then couldn't this lead to neglecting or, more still, even entirely ignoring external things (including one's own body and other people)? He asserts that it is not the business of the philosopher to guard external matters like his wine, his oil, or his body. but rather his own *hēgemonikon*, and then he asks 'how treat externals? Only so far as not to act thoughtlessly about them' (3.10.16). But if our concern is with internals, then why should we not handle externals thoughtlessly? Doesn't considering them as neither 'good' nor 'bad' but rather as morally 'indifferent' to us precisely invite us to waste no thought on them and cast away all worries about how to treat them?

A. The use of externals is not neutral

Epictetus blocks the criticism mentioned above by asserting that although externals are of no intrinsic[6] moral value, the use to which they are put is not at all morally neutral. For example, having learned that the highest of all things is right volition (*prohairesis*), we are urged

... in everything to pursue after this, to be zealous about this, treating all other things as secondary (*parerga*) in comparison with it, though without neglecting these, as far as this is possible. For we must take care of our eyes too, yet not as the highest thing, but we must take care of them for the sake of the highest; because this latter will not be in accordance with nature unless it uses the eyes with reason and chooses one thing instead of another. (2.23.34–5)

My eyes are to be taken care of for the sake of my *prohairesis*, because it is the *prohairesis* which uses all other faculties and parts of the body as instruments for achieving the ends which it sets for itself. Thus all bodily organs and their particular abilities have instrumental, non-moral value. One's own worldly welfare and the welfare of one's loved ones have intrinsic non-moral value, but this value is conditional and not comparable with the unconditional good of the healthy prohairesis (2.23.23–9). In so far as the non-prohairetic faculties are useful as means for achieving prohairetic ends, they have instrumental value. Intrinsic moral goodness and evil, however, are located exclusively in the prohairetic goals (decisions/intentions = *dogmata*) set by the self. The bodily health of the agent has intrinsic, non-moral value, but never unconditional, i.e. moral, value.[7]

The *prohairesis* will be in accord with nature, Epictetus adds, if it uses the body's faculties with reason and selects one thing instead of another. The moral condition of the prohairesis will thus be reflected in how it uses the body's faculties. This additional stipulation that these faculties must be used with reason indicates that the choice of how to use externals (the body itself being an external) is neither unimportant nor arbitrary exactly because the choice derives from the source of all good and evil, the *prohairesis*. If this this were not the case, then Epictetus would certainly be unjustified in claiming that the use of externals matters given his insistence that everything extra-prohairetic is indifferent per se.

Therefore, although the externals themselves as materials are a matter of indifference, the use to which they are put, since it is connected to the *prohairesis,* is not a matter of indifference. Yet this subtle distinction leaves us with the difficult question of how one can use externals with care (since they are 'worthwhile,' *axia*) and yet consider them as morally neutral and thus devoid of intrinsic moral value. Epictetus is quite aware of this difficulty in the following passage, worth quoting at length:

> ... the principal task in life is this: distinguish matters and weigh them one against another and say to yourself, 'Externals are not under my control; volition is under my control. Where am I to look for the good and the evil? Within me, in that which is my own.' But in that which is another's never employ the words 'good' or 'evil,' or 'benefit' or 'injury,' or anything of the sort. What then? Are these externals to be used carelessly? Not at all. For this again is to the volition an evil and thus unnatural to it. They must be used carefully, because their use is not a matter of indifference, and at the same time with steadfastness and peace of mind, because the material is indifferent. For in whatever really concerns us, there no one can either hinder or compel me. The *attainment* of those things in which I can be hindered or compelled is not under my control and is neither good nor bad, but the use which I make of them is either good or bad, and *that* is under my control. It is, indeed, difficult to unite and combine these two things – the carefulness of one devoted to material things and the steadfastness of one who disregards them, but it is not impossible. Otherwise happiness were impossible. (2.5.4–9; emphasis mine)

Happiness, as we see from this passage, is the result of joining the careful use of externals (which directs them toward virtuous ends) with the attitude of secure steadfastness of the agent who knows that her true good, i.e. moral integrity, can in no way be adversely affected by occurrences external to her own personal judgements and choices.

This combination of steadfastness (*eustatheia*) and carefulness (*epimeleia*) is directly parallel to the distinction Epictetus makes when he says that with *ta aprohaireta* one should show confidence (*tharsos*) but with *ta prohairatika* one should show caution (*eulabeia*) (2.1.4). 'For if the evil is in an evil volition, it is only in regard to these matters that it is right to use caution; but if the things that are non-volitional and are not up to us are nothing to us, we ought to employ confidence in regard to them' (2.1.6). The good, conversely, lies in the virtuous exercise of the *prohairesis*. The exercise of the *prohairesis* consists in issuing *dogmata*, the judgements which motivate all our actions, and so it is in making these judgements of how we are to act and how we are to employ externals that we must show caution. All intrinsic moral weight rests on these intentions which we carry into every action we undertake, so with respect to these intentions caution is absolutely required. The results of our actions, on the other hand, are not similarly under our control; they lie outside the domain of our *prohairesis* and so are not determined by it. That is what Epictetus means in 2.5.8 above when he says that the *attainment* of those things in which I can be hindered is not up to me and therefore is neither good nor bad. I cannot guarantee what the results of my actions will be. It is only whether and how I try to act, the 'use which I make of the thing' that is under my control. Thus the material results of the attempted actions, as *ta aprohaireta*, are 'nothing to us,' and so toward them we are free to feel indifferent in as much as we need not worry about the outcome. Since the outcome is beyond our control we are not responsible for it. Good and evil reside exclusively in the attempt: (1) in forming the *dogma* which motivates it and spurs us into action, and (2) in putting our best effort into the action. The resulting success or failure carries no moral weight for the agent.[8]

Epictetus uses an excellent metaphor to illustrate the proper attitude the Stoic should have toward the use of externals. The relation of the agent to externals should be like that of a player toward the equipment of a game. For example, he should imitate those who play dice: 'The counters are indifferent, the dice are indifferent; how am I to know what is going to fall? But to make a careful and skillful use of what has fallen, that is now my task' (2.5.3). The dice are the material equipment of the game, but they are not the object of the game. The object of the game for most non-Stoics is to win. For the Stoic it is to play well in an attempt to win *ceteris paribus*, and this entails using the dice as skillfully as possible. But again, victory itself is beyond the player's control (it is *deo volente*), and so for the Stoic excellence is really to be found in playing as well as one can under the circumstances.

Epictetus also cites the example of playing ball:

> This is what you will see skilful ball players doing also. None of them is concerned about the ball as being something good or bad, but about throwing and catching it. Accordingly, form has to do with that, skill with that, and speed, and grace; where I cannot catch the ball even if I spread out my cloak, the expert catches it if I throw. Yet if we catch or throw the ball in a flurry or in fear, what fun is there left, and how can a man be steady, or see what comes next in the game? But one player will say 'Throw!' another, 'Don't throw!' and yet another, 'Don't throw it up!' That, indeed, would be a strife and not a game. (2.5.15–17)

The player commits his energy to throwing and catching well, gracefully. If it is meant to be, he will pass and catch well. He will not be indifferent to throwing and catching because if he were that would be no game at all. Each play will transpire as it should. If the Stoic player knows the game well, he will work for achieving the game's objectives other things being equal.

Moreover, Epictetus observes above not only that the game is played more skillfully when the players do not play in fear, but that the fun of playing the game is also destroyed by worry and anxiety. One should play the game only as long as it is pleasant to do so (1.25.8). He explains that the ball with which Socrates played during his trial was imprisonment, exile, drinking poison, being deprived of his wife, leaving his children orphans, and he nonetheless played and handled the ball in good form (2.5.19–20).

> So ought we also to act, exhibiting the ballplayer's carefulness about the same, but the same indifference about the object played with, as being a mere ball. For one must by all means strive to show his skill in regard to some of the external materials,

yet without making the material a part of himself, but merely lavishing his skill in regard to it, whatever it may be. (2.5.20–1)

We do not often choose the externals with which we have to play the game, but regardless of what they are we ought to show good form in using them. The good card-player is distinguished not by the cards she happens to be dealt, since that is simply a matter of chance, but by how well she plays her hand.

Now if we take this metaphor seriously, as Epictetus certainly seems to intend, then the Stoic is supposed to view her own body, and even her spouse and children as if they were all like tokens in a game where the playing is what matters. As for the tokens, she '... cares not at all about having, or not having, these things; but, as children playing with potsherds compete with another concerning the game, but take no thought about the potsherds, so this person also has considered the material as nothing, but is glad to play with them and handle them' (4.7.5). To think of one's loved ones as if they were value-neutral game tokens is a chilling thought to say the least. We must remind ourselves here that Epictetus consistently maintains that everything outside one's true self (*prohairesis/hēgemonikon*) including one's body and every other person is not one's own and so must not be claimed as or considered as one's own. This is why he states that 'although life is a matter of indifference, the use which you make of it is not a matter of indifference' (2.6.1). One does not choose to be born, nor does one choose the circumstances into which one is born. Rather one is simply plunged into the life one receives. We do not choose the situations of the game; they are simply thrust upon us. But for Epictetus, winning is not measured by who has which tokens. It is not measured by the tokens at all. Rather, as the cliché goes, it is how you play the game that counts.[9]

So just as the eventual outcome of the game should not be feared since one can be confident one has played it well, confidence is also the very natural consequence of the realization that the outcomes of an agent's actions are beyond her control. She has nothing to fear about them since, in the moral sense, they simply do not matter. They in fact in no way interfere with what is completely within her power to safeguard, namely, her prohairetic matters, i.e. the decisions of her will (*ta dogmata*). Therefore, clearly all events also lie outside one's volition. Now we begin to see how the two following fundamental principles of Epictetus' ethics are connected. '[H]ere are the two principles that you ought to have ready at hand: Outside the volition there is nothing either good or bad; and: We ought not to lead events, but to follow them' (3.10.18). What Epictetus means by 'following events' we now turn to examine.

B. The rationality of following fate

In the previous section it was shown that since the actual outcome of one's action is never guaranteed (since it is beyond the agent's control), Epictetus argues that the agent ought not lose her peace of mind if she meets with failure instead of success in what she tried to achieve. Only what is within her power is the proper object of concern. To desire to have power over what is beyond one's control Epictetus considers to be simply irrational. But not only are the eventual results of one's own actions beyond one's control, but *all* events, *all* occurrences, *all* things which happen external to one's own *prohairesis* are also beyond one's control and are consequently neither good nor bad but indifferent. 'Whenever some disturbing news is reported to you, have this at hand: News about the volition never occurs' (3.18.1), and so since news does not pertain to one's moral responsibility, it should not be disturbing. Thus there is no justified reason for being disturbed by any event. To become upset by any extra-prohairetic event is to forget the fundamental division between what is and what is not one's own, and then to want that which is not one's own to *be* one's own. 'There is but one way to serenity (keep this thought ready for use at dawn. and by day, and at night), and that is to yield up all claim to the non-volitional things, to regard nothing as your own possession; to surrender everything to the deity, to fortune' (4.4.39). The rational acceptance that all things outside one's *prohairesis* are essentially beyond one's control and so not part of one's true self, and the consequent judgement that they are not to be claimed or clung to at even the least sacrifice of one's dignity, virtue, or moral integrity – this is the one way to serenity.

Once one has firmly grasped the truth of the judgement that what is beyond one's control lies entirely outside the realm of one's moral responsibility, then one can judge that from a *moral* standpoint any result, outcome, event, occurrence, or happening is utterly indifferent. For Epictetus, since they are *morally* indifferent they are at most only of conditional concern. This conclusion can be drawn on entirely secular grounds; it is free of any theological or cosmological presuppositions.

To convince us that no course of events prevents us from producing the correct *dogmata* which allow us to live in accordance with nature, i.e. virtuously, is according to Epictetus just what the philosopher does. 'To what end, then, do philosophers have precepts to offer? – To this end, that whatever happens, our governing principle shall be, and abide to the end, in accord with nature' (3.9.11). The philosopher's *hegemonikon*, because it is equipped with correct judgements, is not disturbed or upset by worldly happenings, since whatever these happenings may be, the philosopher can conform his desires and aversions accordingly:

> ... we picture the work of the philosopher to be something like this: He should bring his own will (*boulēsis*) into harmony with what happens, so that neither anything that happens happens against our will (*akontōn hēmōn*), nor anything that fails to happen fails to happen when we wish it to happen. The result of this for those who have so ordered the work of philosophy is that in desire they are not disappointed, and in aversion they do not fall into what they would avoid ... (2.14.7–8)

Here we see Epictetus extending his reasoning about what our attitude toward happenings ought to be. Not only should we view what happens in the external, extra-prohairetic world as indifferent, but the philosopher is the one who has trained himself[10] to accept and embrace all happenings. He in fact wants only what does actually happen to happen: 'Do not seek to have everything that happens happen as you wish, but wish for everything to happen as it actually does happen, and your life will be serene' (*Ench.* 8). This is because 'the origin of sorrow is this – to wish for something that does not come to pass' (1.27.10).

Here Epictetus has moved from arguing that since external events need not disturb one's *prohairesis* one need not worry or care about them (one may view them as indifferent), to making the stronger claim that the philosopher in fact *wants* events to happen as they do. He has gone beyond inferring that the Stoic is justified in being apathetic about fate to asserting that the Stoic is positively pleased with whatever fate brings.

Although this unconditional affirmation of every twist and turn of fate would strike most as such an extreme form of optimistic fatalism as to severely strain the bounds of psychological realism, for Epictetus it follows quite naturally from traditional Stoic precepts. Epictetus, like his early Stoic predecessors, believed that *orthos logos* pervaded the whole universe. Each event is thus fateful in that it unfolds according to the rationality of the whole. Thus a divine providence steers all events. 'Whenever you find fault with providence (*pronoia*), only consider and you will recognize that what happens is in accordance with reason (*kata logon*)' (3.17.1). Therefore, since each and every event is in this sense rational, and '[t]o the rational being only the irrational is unendurable, but the rational is endurable' (1.2.1), every event, no matter what it may be, is endurable to the rational being, e.g. the true philosopher.

This supposition that fate is rational, however, rests on the common belief of the Greeks that the *kosmos* is a rational order. For the Stoics, this meant that each particular event within the *kosmos* on a microscopic scale reflects the eminently rational organization of the whole on the macroscopic scale. Epictetus staunchly holds this belief because he holds the orthodox Stoic view that Zeus is the perfectly rational orderer of the *kosmos*, and that he has constituted the world and ordained the entire course of nature so as to unfold, even down to the smallest occurrence, in complete accordance with reason.

The benefits of belief in the rationality of fate are the peace of mind and mental freedom which, for Epictetus, constitute real happiness. When one conforms one's desires to the governance of Zeus, obeys it, and is well satisfied with it, one never suffers misfortune, ill fortune, or blames anyone (2.23.42). There is no such thing as bad luck or misfortune since *every* event happens just as Zeus, in his supreme rationality, wants it to. Epictetus' reasoning is that one is only compelled if one resists fate by wanting events to occur other than they do: 'in a word, give up wanting anything but what god wants. And who will prevent you, who will compel you? No one, any more than anyone prevents or compels Zeus' (2.17.22). Just as Zeus' will can never be hindered, by aligning her own mind, as it were, to that of Zeus the true philosopher can say:

> But I have never been hindered in the exercise of my will (*thelōn*), nor have I ever been subjected to compulsion against my will (*mē thelōn*). And how is this possible? I have submitted my impulse-to-choose (*tēn hormēn*) unto god. He wills that I shall have fever; it is my will too. He wills that I should have an impulse (*horman*) for something; it is my will too. He wills that I should desire something; it is my will too. He wills that I should get something; I want it (*boulomai*) too. He does not will it; I do not want it. (4.1.89)

This passage reveals what is arguably the most problematic feature of the Stoic worldview.[11] Here Epictetus seems to contradict his own account of assent, desire, and choice (see Chapter 1). That Zeus can will (determine) that Epictetus' body succumbs to a fever is unproblematic since his body, as an external, is not essentially under his control. Thus if it is subjected to a fever it is god's will that it be so. In this case it makes sense for Epictetus to say he submits his impulse-to-choose (*hormē*) unto god. But Epictetus' assent (*sunkatathesis*), unlike his body, is the fundamental thing which god has made 'up to him' and thus his assent is not subject to anyone else *including* god. Freedom, on the Stoic account, is to be located in the act of assent. For the early Stoics, assent is to the lekton: 'Action X is to be done by me now.' Epictetus formulates this idea by speaking of the *prohairesis* forming the *dogma* which motivates the action. The agent's choice of *dogmata* (or the applied use of *phantasiai*) involved in determining one's hormetic impulse to act is not within Zeus' power (cf. 1.1.23 and 1.17.27). For Epictetus to suggest in 4.1.89 that a person's choices/assents come from anywhere other than that person's own self clearly indicates a mistake of expression by Epictetus. An agent's choices/ assents cannot be hindered (far less determined) by any extra-prohairetic source. As Bonhöffer correctly observes, Epictetus 'constantly proclaims the independence of the mind from the conditions of the body without any restriction. In every *peristasis* the person can keep his *hēgemonikon* in accordance with nature, and the endurance of pain and of illness is according to Epictetus a completely sufficient moral aim of life.'[12] For Epictetus the individual's freedom of assent is absolute. A charitable interpretation of 4.1.89 would be that Epictetus conforms his will to Zeus' in that he accepts what Zeus wills he get or not get.[13]

Epictetus explains what he means by 'submitting his *hormē* unto god' consistently with his more tenable doctrine later on in this same chapter: Thus he reflects and comes to the thought that, if he attach himself to god, he will pass through the world in safety. How do you mean 'attach himself'? – Why, so that whatever god wills, he also wills, and whatever god does not will, this he also does not will. (4.1.98–9). Here Epictetus displays a much more acceptable account of how desiring what god desires works. The agent 'attaches himself to god' by conforming his will to each external *event* as it happens. The agent does not receive his *desire* from god and then conform his will to it (as 4.1.89 appeared to indicate).

In conditionally seeking a 'worthwhile thing' (*axia*), the Stoic is again conforming his will to Zeus. In what sense, then, does the Stoic want to drink water when thirsty? He drinks it believing that it has some positive, practical value for him. Before he acts, he attributes this value to the action in the belief that he should drink instead of not drinking. This attributed, provisional value is a *conditional* value. It is conditional upon its being fated by Zeus that he does, in fact, ingest the water. If it is not so fated, then he will reject the initial, provisional attribution of value. In the way the

Stoic 'wants' the water, he wants it conditionally upon Zeus' will before the fact, and after he does not get the water he conforms his will to Zeus' by not being disturbed by the failure to ingest the water. It was so fated, after all, that he go thirsty on that particular occasion.

The Stoic has the faith that whatever will happen will occur as Zeus ordains, and this faith in the rationality of future events certainly gives rise to his feeling of confident expectation. Epictetus explains how, armed with the Stoic attitude, he can no longer fear the rebuff of chamberlains.

> Why, then, do you go to the gate of the palace? – Because I think it fitting for me to join in the game while the game lasts. – How, then, is it that you are locked out? (Oldfather's note: That is, it cannot properly be said of a man that he is 'locked out' if he does not 'wish' to enter.) – Because, if anyone will not receive me, I do not want (*ou thelō*) to go in, but always I want the thing which takes place. For I regard what the god wants as better than what I want. As a servant and follower I shall attach myself to him, choose with him, desire with him, in a word, will with him (*sunormō, sunoregomai, hapōs suntheō*). (4.7.19–20)

This important passage requires extensive commentary. The idea of playing one's role in a game or within the context of a rule-guided activity is often reiterated by Epictetus. The Stoic's position in the world is like the soldier stationed at her post (3.24.31–6); her behavior is to be guided by her assigned military duties. Epictetus also uses the simile of the polite banquet guest (*Ench.* 15; cf. 4.7.21–4) whose gustatory conduct should be guided by rules of dinner party etiquette. The skillful ball-player (2.5.15–20), the shrewd dice-player (2.5.3), and the mindful bather (*Ench.* 4) are other examples Epictetus uses. The Stoic is situated in the world like the passenger of a ship on a sea-voyage (2.5.10–12 and cf. *Ench.* 7). the traveller at an inn (*Ench.* 11), and the actor of a stageplay (*Ench.* 17). The idea in all of these analogies is that the person ought to participate in the activity at hand and do what is within her power to do, i.e. what is incumbent upon her, in the context of that activity without worrying about that activity ending, the behavior of others, or any affairs other than the one in which she is engrossed.

It seems to me that there are two distinct concepts at work in Epictetus although they are difficult to separate because he tends to slide from one to the other. We can distinguish between (a) the cosmological rationality of what happens, and (b) the theological, divine, fateful providence of events. The secular notion (a) is that there is a reason for each event which is embedded in the inherent nature and intrinsic constitution of each object. The universe is an organic unity which functions according to a principle of cosmic order, i.e. a regularity of nature.[14]

The theological view (b) extrapolates beyond the immanent coherence of the world-order to a quasi-transcendent conception of *theos* as 'God' – a personal divinity who is ordainer and paternal provider of all. This view conceives of *orthos logos* as centered in a particular supreme being instead of pervading an impersonal yet organically integrated universe. View (b) is manifested in Epictetus' description in 4.7.20 of the wise philosopher who attaches himself to god and wishes only for what does happen in the belief that god's will is better than his own. When he says that he chooses-with (*sunormō*) desires-with (*sunoregomai*) and wills-together-with (*sunthelō*) god, we could interpret this to mean that what the god desires to happen, he too desires to happen, that what god chooses to happen, he too chooses to happen. Epictetus staunchly believes that what is best for a person is whatever god pleases to have happen to that person (2.7.13). Without this conviction that god's will is better than her own, the Stoic's *amor fati* would be unfounded. Yet if the Stoic feels no need to justify the universe in the first place, then she need not resort to any theological speculation whatsoever.

Epictetus elaborates on why it is rational to want what god wants by comparing desiring what seems best to *me* to happen with desiring to write the name 'Dio' as I choose. This is to turn the situation backwards. Rather, he observes, I am taught to desire to write it as it ought to be written (1.12.11–13). And god knows better than we do how things ought to be; so

... instruction consists precisely in learning to desire each thing exactly as it happens. And how do they happen? As he that ordains them has ordained. And he has ordained that there be summer and winter, and abundance and dearth, and virtue and vice, and all such opposites, for the harmony of the whole, and he has given each of us a body, and members of the body, and property and companions. Mindful, therefore, of this ordaining we should go to receive instruction, not in order to change the constitution of things, for this is neither vouchsafed us nor is it better that it should be, but in order that, things about us being as they are and as their nature is, we may, for our own part, keep our intents (*gnōmē*) in harmony with what happens. (1.12.15–17)

The preset constitution of things contains its own rationality so we should not want to meddle with it, but ought to recognize it and conform our minds to it. In this respect the message of the secular view (a) is that as rational beings we can attune our attitudes so as to participate in 'the harmony of the whole.' Yet we see again in this passage Epictetus' belief that there is one who *ordains* that nature be as it is. This personification of cosmic *logos* in view (b) may represent a new form of piety which, of course, the early Christians will pick up on. In any case, Stoic instruction consists in accepting the events of and in nature and patterning our mental outlook in harmony with how events actually do unfold.

A second point emerges from 1.12.15–17, 4.1.98–9, and 4.7.20. The will as a distinct mental power as we moderns understand it, which is certainly not present in Aristotle, is beginning to emerge in the late Stoics. *Voluntas* is a key term for Seneca which basically corresponds to *prohairesis* for Epictetus.

Epictetus recognizes that the Stoic's optimistic fatalism is difficult to maintain. Some events appear to be real adversities that we cannot bring ourselves to embrace cheerfully and positively affirm. Yet in these cases Epictetus reminds us that we can at least bear fate by calling upon our mental resources.

Come, have you not received faculties that enable you to bear whatever happens? Have you not received magnanimity? Have

you not received courage? Have you not received endurance?
And what do I care any longer for anything that may happen,
if I be magnanimous? What shall perturb me, or trouble me, or
seem grievous to me? Shall I fail to use my faculty to that end for
which I have received it, but grieve and lament over events that
occur? (1.6.28–9 and cf. 2.16.14)

God has so arranged our human nature that we are free to bear all
– even the vicissitudes of fate which *appear* to be most negative. Of
course they so appear to us[15] only because we are unable to discern
their underlying appropriateness and rationality:

> ... god has not merely given us these faculties, to enable us to
> bear all that happens without being degraded or crushed thereby,
> but, as became a good king and in very truth a father, he has
> given them to us free from all restraint, compulsion, hindrance;
> he has put the whole matter under our control without reserving
> even for himself any power to prevent or hinder. (1.6.40; cf. also
> 1.29.39)

In other words, god has empowered us to bear up under all strokes
of fate which he, in his supreme wisdom, sees fit to ordain. God[16]
has so made us that we can endure any event if only we resolve to.

But since we are so endowed as to endure these things without being
disturbed by them, god has made us thereby capable of preserving our
happiness. As for the death of your son, the loss of your ship, being
imprisoned, etc. god 'has made you capable of patient endurance,
and high-minded, because he has taken from these things the quality
of being evils, because you are permitted to suffer these things and
still to be happy...' (3.8.6). Since all these events are beyond one's
control and lie outside one's volition (*prohairesis*), they are not evils
and so cannot in themselves affect one's happiness.

Epictetus moreover believes that the reflective individual has the
capacity positively to praise fate:

> From everything that happens in the universe it is easy to find
> occasion to praise providence, if one has within himself these

two qualities: the faculty of taking a comprehensive view of what has happened in each individual instance, and the sense of gratitude. Otherwise, one will not see the usefulness of what has happened, and another, even if he does see it, will not be grateful for it. (1.6.1–2)

Once again, with the proper mental resources (in this case the global view and gratitude) Epictetus is confident that every event can be interpreted as useful for some end and therefore deserving of thankfulness. What is so remarkable about this attitude of gratitude is that Epictetus believes it can be maintained in the face of what are commonly considered to be the most tragic, horrible adversities. He asserts it is possible to derive benefit from *everything*, regardless of how harmful and wretched the non-Stoic thinks it is:

> [b]ring whatever you will and *I* will turn it into a good. Bring disease, bring death, bring poverty, reviling, peril of life in court; all these things will become helpful at a touch from the magic wand of Hermes. 'What will you make of death?' Why, what else but make it your glory, or an opportunity for you to show in deed thereby what sort of person one is who follows the purpose (*boulēma*) of nature. 'What will you make of disease?' I will show its character, I will shine in it, I will be firm, I will be serene. I will not fawn upon my physician, I will not pray for death. What else do you still seek? Everything that you give I will turn into something blessed, productive of happiness, august, enviable. (3.20.12–15)[17]

Epictetus goes on to say that once he gets the right idea of a thing (death, disease, poverty, not holding office, etc.) it can no longer hurt him. All of these so-called hardships can be viewed as opportunities for displaying his virtues and strength of character since they are the materials for his *prohairesis* (1.29.2–3). His fortitude and serenity can shine through even when illness debilitates his body. Once he understands the nature of disease he knows that it only affects his body but does not prevent him from preserving his inner moral composure. Following Socrates, Epictetus calls death and hardship 'bugbears' (*mormolukeia*) – once one has examined them and learned what they are, one will understand that they themselves are not truly fearful, but the fear of hardship or death is the truly fearful thing since that fear leads one to act disgracefully (2.1.13–20 and 3.26.38). He observes that since every living being must die sooner or later, if one simply cannot find profit from a perceived hardship then 'the door stands open,' i.e. suicide always allows one to exit from her trouble (2.1.20).[18]

Epictetus himself, however, believes that no 'hardship' is completely devoid of profit, and thus that one can bear them all. 'What, then, ought one say to oneself at each hardship that befalls him? "It was for this that I kept training, it was to meet this that I used to practise"', (3.10.7). Each perceived hardship represents an occasion to test one's Stoic strength, i.e. one's mental composure and moral fortitude (cf. also 1.24.1–2). The Stoic trains herself to endure just such occasions by means of applying her reason to the individual cases, learning their nature, and realizing they do not impugn her moral character. So-called hardships are simply god's way of training the individual to maintain her virtue no matter what (3.24.113).

Because of this unshakable confidence that any event whatsoever can be turned into something which strengthens one's character and so is beneficial to one's mental resilience, Epictetus' view about 'good fortune' is that the individual has the power to create it for herself.

> Don't say 'I'm miserable, that this has befallen me!' but rather, 'I'm fortunate, because although this has befallen me, I continue to live untroubled, being neither crushed by the present nor afraid of the future.' For something of this kind might have befallen anyone; but not everyone would have continued to live untroubled by it. Why, then, count the former aspect of the matter a misfortune, rather than this latter good fortune? And in general do you call a human's misfortune that which is not an aberration from human nature? And does that seem to you to be an aberration from human nature which does not contravene

the purpose (*boulēma*) of his nature? What then? This purpose you have already learned; this, then, which has befallen you does not prevent you, does it, from being just, high-minded, self-controlled, self-possessed, deliberate, free from deceit, self-respecting, free, and everything else, the possession of which enables the nature of the human to come into its own?[19]

Only something contrary to the nature of a human being would be a true misfortune, but since all the virtues listed above belong to human nature and allow one to take the *supposedly* miserable event in one's stride while maintaining one's composure, one can view it as fortunate that we are so equipped by nature as to remain steadfast come what may. Thus, for Epictetus, to bear any event nobly and well is true good fortune.

Knowing she has this steadfastness at her disposal the Stoic has no fear of the future. For the Stoic nothing could possibly bode ill: '... for me every portent is favorable, if I so wish (*thelō*); for whatever be the outcome, it is within my power to derive benefit from it' (*Ench.* 18). She is free to employ her natural faculties so as to turn any future outcome to good personal use.

> Isn't the future now non-volitional? – Yes. – And is not the essence (*ousia*) of the good and evil in volitional things? – Yes. – Are you permitted, then, to make a natural use of every outcome? No one can prevent you, can he? – No one. – Therefore, no longer say to me, 'How is it to happen?' Because, whatever happens, you'll make good of it, and the outcome will be a blessing for you. (4.10.8–9)

In this way the Stoic creates her own blessing, her own good fortune. '[H]aving first made up your mind that every issue is indifferent and nothing to you, but that, whatever it may be, it will be possible for you to turn it to good use, and that no one will prevent this' (*Ench.* 32.2). Nothing and no one prevents the Stoic from converting what may seem to be a hardship or adversity into something useful or beneficial to her except her own decision to grieve and lament over it. It is completely within her power to employ her natural faculties and virtues so as to direct every outcome to good purpose; only her own inability to discern the rationality and moral harmlessness of the event bars her from turning it to her own advantage. We can suppose that it is this sort of lack of understanding that makes one too weak to bear a particular event and thus opt for suicide (as in 2.1.20).

To review, then, Epictetus gives at least five different reasons why one should not be disturbed by any event, outcome, or happening, past, present, or future: (1) since any worldly occurrence is external to one's own *prohairesis*, it is neither good nor bad but indifferent; (2) natural events are rational, and to the rational being the rational is always endurable (hence secular view (a)); (3) Zeus ordains everything that happens and his providence is superior to what I will, so I can keep my mind in harmony with fate by conforming my will to his divine intent (hence theological view (b)); (4) I am so equipped that I am free to bear all that happens without being disturbed; (5) it is possible to turn every event into something beneficial, e.g. by using it to strengthen one's patience, magnanimity, fortitude, resilience and the like.

Thus when Epictetus lays down as the second principle that we ought to have ready at hand that 'We ought not to lead events, but to follow them,' we can safely interpret this to mean that we ought to follow events with our desire: we should not expect or wish for future events to conform to our desires – to 'lead events' in this way would be vain and foolish. Rather, we should remind ourselves that whatever happens we can conform our desire and apply our abilities in order to cope with all events and put them to good use. Epictetus certainly does not mean that we ought to be passive spectators of life who let ourselves be swept along by the course of events. I suggest that Epictetus simply means that we ought to accept whatever happens and remain confident that we will be able to act in such a way as to maintain our moral integrity successfully and in so doing preserve our mental harmony.[20]

C. Do your best and accept the rest

In section A of this chapter we examined how Epictetus maintains that although externals are, as mere materials for virtue, of no intrinsic moral value and thus in themselves 'indifferent,' the use of externals reflects the moral condition of the self and so is of great importance. In section B we saw how Epictetus infers that any and all outcomes of actions are strictly speaking beyond our control (as *ta aprohaireta*), so that the intention and attempt to act and not the consequent attainment of the attempted action are all that matter morally. We are responsible only for what is 'up to us,' what is under our control, namely, *ta dogmata*, the judgements we make, the decisions of our *prohairesis*. Our good lies exclusively in this prohairetic sphere, which is completely under our control. But all else is not completely and not essentially under our control, so in the extra-prohairetic sphere we can only try to affect things as best we can. 'Guard your own good in everything you do; and for the rest be content to take simply what has been given you, in so far as you can make a rational use of it' (4.3.11). Whatever externals we find in our possession do not strictly belong to us, since, for Epictetus, they are not part of our real self. But we should be content to have them and we are free to make a rational use of them, even though we are not free to possess them for ever or guarantee the results of our attempted rational utilization.[21]

Here it is helpful to return to the game metaphor discussed earlier. We are free to use the game tokens that we happen to have to the best of our ability. The skill of our playing is displayed in how well we handle them. As De Lacy writes: 'Viewed in this light, life is a game. The rules and conditions are set up, and it is the player's duty to follow these conditions as best he can. The apparatus employed in the game have no intrinsic value'.[22] However, the tokens themselves have their own inherent particular natures, and our play cannot alter them. Nor does my play alone ensure victory for me, since the play of the other players as well as the incidental conditions of the game itself (all factors beyond my control) also contribute to the determination of the final outcome. This is what

Epictetus means when he says: 'We must make the best of what is under our control, and take the rest as its nature is. "How, then, is its nature?" As the god wills (*thelēi*)' (1.1.17; cf. 4.13.24).

If we understand the nature of the situational circumstances of the activity in which we are participating, then we can try to manage as well[23] as possible those parts that we can affect and still accept whatever may ensue. By remembering the nature of the enterprise one can keep one's mind in harmony with its natural results.

> When you are on the point of putting your hand to some under-taking, remind yourself what the nature of that undertaking is. If you are going out of the house to bathe, put before your mind what happens at a public bath – those who splash you with water, those who jostle against you, those who vilify you and rob you. And thus you will set about your undertaking more securely if at the outset you say to yourself, 'I want (*thelō*) to take a bath, and, at the same time, to keep my volition in harmony with nature.' And so do in every undertaking. For thus, if anything happens to hinder you in your bathing, you will be ready to say, 'Oh, well, this was not the only thing that I wanted, but I wanted also to keep my volition in harmony with nature; and I shall not so keep it if I am vexed at what is going on.' (*Ench.* 4)

The Stoic should want to bathe with the right kind of reservations about bathhouse nuisances which could, if she let them, endanger the well-disposed, orderly state of her *prohairesis*. Zeus has made the bather so that she is free to keep her self *kata phusin*, but to do so she must not fight against how Zeus (god) wills things should be. Mental harmony requires acceptance of whatever happens.

Epictetus believes that accepting the natural division between 'what is one's own' (internals) and 'what is not one's own' (externals), and not only being content with what externals one happens to have been given while at the same time not desiring any other externals, but also, upon losing those externals which one does have, to relinquish them without grief or hesitation and feel grateful for having them at all as long as one did – all this Epictetus believes is a matter of divine ordinance.

And what is the law (*nomos*) of god? To guard what is his own, not to lay claim to what is not his own, but to make use of what is given him, and not to yearn for what has not been given; when something is taken away, to give it up readily and without delay, being grateful for the time in which he had the use of it. (2.16.28)

So we have the responsibility of making good, rational use of whatever externals happen to come into our possession, according to Epictetus, and we should appreciate them while we have them. We can and ought to enjoy externals for as long as god sees fit for us to have them. But since we not only receive everything, even our very self, from god, and it is also he, in his supreme wisdom, who takes away external things from us (4.1.100–110), Epictetus holds that we should appreciate them when we have them. Yet we ought never to attach ourselves to externals so we will not be disturbed by their loss.

This is a difficult point in Epictetus' Stoic ethics because it is hard to see how one could appreciate or delight in a thing without thereby valuing it as a full-blooded good which really does contribute to one's happiness (*eudaimonia*). Bonhöffer attempts to explain Epictetus' position as follows:

Although Epictetus seriously emphasizes the worthlessness of external goods for true happiness, yet he values them as by no means entirely trifling, but means to please himself with their possession and enjoyment so long as it is offered. The apathy which he demands is, I would like to say, not a psychological but only a moral one: whoever does not possess these external goods should not desire them and when he loses them should not mourn and complain over it, because thereby the inner peace is disturbed and the moral aim of life is missed. But whoever has them is allowed to be pleased with them and must thank God for it. Nothing is more offensive to our philosopher or is able to irritate him more than a dissatisfied, ungrateful mind which does not recognize and appreciate the gifts of god.[24]

Thus Bonhöffer accurately enough portrays Epictetus as calling exclusively for the positive enjoyment of externals while rejecting any and all negative responses toward their absence. Yet I fail to see how his distinction between psychological and moral apathy succeeds in rescuing Epictetus from the following difficulty. On Epictetus' own account, if something is beneficial or useful or profitable to someone, then that person perforce desires to have it and is frustrated if she cannot have it. She is naturally disturbed by the loss of a worthwhile thing. But if one is grateful for having had a worthwhile thing, then isn't one also disappointed in having it no longer? If one truly enjoys, appreciates, and delights in the use of an external while one has it, then how can one feel gratitude for the time one used to have it without also feeling disappointment for not having it in the present? Unless it ceased to have practical or aesthetic worth the moment the individual lost it, it is difficult to see how the individual could feel grateful for having had it without also desiring to have it again.

In any case, Epictetus himself believes that gratitude for and positive delight in the 'gifts of god' that one happens to have are possible without at all missing them as real 'goods' in their absence.[25] The Stoic is allowed to feel delight (*chara*) in an external since it is a 'good-feeling' (*eupatheia*) which is not at all disturbing to the soul. Nevertheless, no external is strictly considered 'good' (*agathon*), but at most only 'worthwhile' (*axia*).

As we saw in Chapter 1, Epictetus definitely thinks that one can uphold an attitude of gratitude toward each and every event. The temporary use of an external could be appreciated because as a thing that is 'not one's own', to have it at all for any time is neither to be expected nor to be counted on. Still, Epictetus insists it is wrong to attach oneself to any external because it is simply a fact that it is not one's own. By attaching oneself to god instead of to any external one can completely avoid disappointment at its loss and yet be grateful for having had it.

On the whole, Epictetus wants to take a deflationary attitude toward externals. They are in themselves indifferent, i.e. morally insignificant. Pursuit and avoidance pertain to volition, while ordinary decisions about externals are matters for *eklogē* (selection/

preference), i.e. 'using the material.' Selection of externals ought never to cost the least sacrifice of one's own[26] moral character, dignity, or integrity (cf. *Ench.* 24.3). Epictetus shows this by explaining that the distribution of honorary posts, money, and prestigious offices is to be conceived of as if somebody were scattering dried figs and nuts; the Stoic should let others scramble to snatch them up.

> But what, then, if, when they are being thrown about, a dried fig chances to fall into my lap? I take it up and eat it. For I may properly value even a dried fig as much as that. But neither a dried fig, nor any other of the things not good, which the philosophers have persuaded me not to think good, is worth my grovelling and upsetting someone else, or being upset by him, or flattering those who have flung the dried figs among us. (4.7.24)

Government posts, offices, and money are mere trifles that can be put to rational use (like eating dried figs), yet they should not be frantically sought, but only calmly accepted if they happen to fall into one's lap. As externals they should be skillfully used (consumed), but they should be properly esteemed for what they are (in this case, figs are just desserts).

In this next passage Epictetus illustrates how true friends want my congenial respect, not a share of my moneys.

> 'Get money, then,' says some friend, 'in order that we too may have it.' If I can get money and at the same time keep myself self-respecting, and faithful, and high-minded, show me the way and I will get it. But if you require me to lose the good things that belong to me, in order that you may acquire the things that are not good, you can see for yourselves how unfair and inconsiderate you are. And which do you want more? Money, or a faithful and self-respecting friend? Help me, therefore, rather to this end, and do not require me to do those things which will make me lose those qualities. (*Ench.* 24.3)

Money, like all material items, is not a true good, so it too is not worth having at the smallest loss of one's dignified integrity (a true good). The Vietnam POW Vice Admiral James Bond Stockdale, USN, applied *Ench.* 24.3 to his own situation: 'To love our fellow prisoners was within our power. To betray, to propagandize, to disillusion conscientious and patriotic shipmates and destroy their morale so that they in turn would be destroyed was to lose one's proper good'.[27] For Stockdale and Viktor E. Frankl,[28] Stoicism worked in an environment of extortion. For these two men of the twentieth century, at least, self-disciplined integrity produced spiritual invulnerability even, or perhaps especially, in the midst of grave physical peril and prolonged stressful crisis.

In the following passage Epictetus draws the crucial distinction between the good of the body and the good (here the social amenity) of the self:

> [F]or you to take (*eklegō*) the larger share is worthwhile (*axia*) for your body; still, it is detrimental (*apaxia*) for the maintenance of the social feeling (*koinōnikon*) at a banquet. When, therefore, you are eating with another person, remember to regard, not merely the worth (*axia*) for your body of what lies before you, but also to maintain your respect for your host. (*Ench.* 36)

The message here is clear: one ought not to compromise the proper fulfillment of one's role as a polite guest in order to indulge one's gluttony.[29]

He uses the prosaic food metaphor again to depict how one ought not to lose one's patient decorum.

> Remember that you ought to behave in life as you would at a banquet. As something is being passed around it comes to you; stretch out your hand and take a portion of it politely. It passes on; do not detain it. Or it has not come to you yet; do not project your desire to meet it, but wait until it comes in front of you. So act toward children, so toward a wife, so toward office, so toward wealth; and then some day you will be worthy of the banquets of the gods. (*Ench.* 15)

Epictetus then adds the austere remark: 'But if you do not take these things even when they are set before you, but despise them, then you will not only share the banquet of the gods, but share also their rule' (*Ench.* 15). That this despising of external goods is actually a superhuman accomplishment is clear from the last sentence of this paragraph: 'For it was by doing so that Diogenes and Herakleitos, and men like them, were deservedly divine and deservedly so called.' The Stoic evidently differs from the Cynic on exactly this point. The Cynic is so totally self-sufficient that he is even happy to refrain from the common indulgences of life. The Stoic does not turn away from the 'gifts of god' as the ascetic Cynic does. To limit oneself to accepting calmly the externals which come one's way is admirably noble (and this is just what the Stoic does). To abstain from all but the most meager material necessities is more than noble: it is divine and hence is characteristic of the Cynic and perhaps[30] also the celebrated super-Stoic, the sage.

Epictetus quite effectively uses his metaphor of the inn to display the proper Stoic attitude toward externals. Just as when stopping at a nice inn in a foreign land one should not stay there permanently but continue on to one's home country, so should one also not cling to and be distracted by nice externals, but rather proceed directly to the prompt fulfillment of one's duties (2.23.36). Externals in my possession are not to be regarded as really 'mine,' i.e. parts of my true self, but merely as things temporarily in my use that belong to another, like the bed I occupy (rent) in an inn (1.24.14). Since, then, every external is given to you and taken from you by 'the giver' (*ho dous*), '[s]o long as he gives it to you, take care of it as of a thing that is not your own, as travellers treat their inn' (*Ench.* 11). This attitude equally pertains to all people since they too are externals. But because of the individual's natural relations to family, friends, community, and country, we will see in the next chapter that she is situated in such a way as to have specific duties toward these externals.

Notes

1. Bonhöffer (1894: 43) correctly observes that Epictetus does not use the terms '*proēgmenon*' and '*apoproēgmenon*,' but operates entirely with the same concepts. He is correct to say that for Epictetus externals are indifferent in so far as they contribute nothing to the happiness or unhappiness of the individual, and that some externals have a relative value while others have a disvalue (the former being relatively according to nature, the latter being contrary to nature). Epictetus' concern is to emphasize that all externals *as a group* are of no importance at all compared to moral matters. Within the class of indifferents which are *kata phusin* he does not rank externals so that they have varying degrees of worth relative to each other, as 'relative value' may suggest. I think it more salutary to describe the value of externals which are *kata phusin* as possessing conditional, provisional, and instrumental worth. Epictetus' innovation is to concentrate on how the use of externals may be according to nature (and reason) or contrary to nature (and reason), and this is determined by the context in which and the purpose for which they are used (as is clear from 2.5.24). As I will try to show, Epictetus circumvents difficulties that would arise from considering those externals with instrumental, conditional worth as possessing differing grades of intrinsic value – that is, value independently of and without relation to the art of living of any human being. Epictetus focuses on the use of externals made by the *prohairesis*. Understood in this way, one can correctly say externals have value only in relation to the *prohairesis*. What is morally indifferent is thus nevertheless 'of concern' as is evidenced by the notion of *epimeleia*.

2. I thank John Cooper for clarifying this distinction.

3. Namely 2.6.9–10; in addition cf. 2.5.10: 'What is possible for me? To select (*eklexasthai*) the helmsman, the sailors, the day, the moment'; and 2.10.6: 'But as it is, seeing that we do not know beforehand what is going to happen, it is incumbent upon us to cleave to that which is is naturally more fit to be

selected (*eklogē*), since we are born for this purpose.' See also Voelke (1973: 65–72).

4. 'All material goods and bads, all which are contrary to our passions, are purely imaginary goods and bads; only that which depends on us is good or bad, all which does not depend on us is indifferent. This postulate is the key to the entire morality of Epictetus who announces it with the most intransigent clarity *abandoning the theory of 'preferables'* by which traditional Stoicism had wanted to distinguish finely a formula which could appear too emphatic' (Le Hir, 1954: 75); my emphasis. This is Stephen R. Morris' translation of: 'Tous les biene et les maux matériels, tout ce qui favorise ou contrarie nos passions, sont des biens et des maux purement imaginaires; seul ce qui dépend de nous est bon ou mauvais, tout ce qui ne dépend pas de nous est indifférent. Ce postulat est la clef de toute la morale d'Épictète, qui l'énonce avec la netteté la plus intransigeante, abandonnant la théorie des 'préférables,' par laquelle le stoicisme moyen avait voulu nuancer une formule qui pouvait paraître trop tranchante.'

5. 'But he [Epictetus] knew that the relative valuation of the "things according to nature" had led to many difficulties and compromise solutions within his school. ... That is the reason why he himself prefers a bipartition which admits no intermediate grade' (Pohlenz, 1948: 329–30). This is my translation of: 'Aber er wußte, daß die relative Bewertung der "naturgemäßen Dinge" zu manchen Schwierigkeiten und Kompromißlosungen innerhalb seiner Schule gefuhrt hatte. ... Daher bevorzugte er selbst eine Zweiteilung, die keine Mittelstufe vertrug.' As in note 1 above, if Pohlenz means that Epictetus makes no gradations of value *within* the class of indifferents *kata phusin* relative to one another, then he is correct. If, however, Pohlenz is denying that Epictetus operates implicitly with the distinction between those externals which are *kata phusin* and therefore *ceteris paribus* choiceworthy, and those which are *para phusin* and therefore usually but only conditionally to be dispreferred, his interpretation is incorrect.

6. By 'intrinsic' I mean *ceteris paribus* choiceworthy in itself.

7. That Epictetus does not discount all non-prohairetic faculties as worthless, nor disparage the study of rhetoric, the analysis of syllogisms, etc. is clear when he says 'Yet I am not disparaging this, but only the habit of dwelling unceasingly on these matters and setting one's hopes in them' (2.23.46). He does not want the pursuit of these matters to distract one from concentrating on prohairetic concerns. Rather, he wants to urge that the former must always be used for and subordinated to the latter. For Epictetus' use of logic see Barnes (1997), Chapter 3.

8. 'Since the wise man is interested only in conformity with nature, the success or failure of his actions in respect of their expected results will be indifferent to him – not in the sense that he does not try to achieve them at all, but in the sense that the outcome of his actions, which must have been ordained by nature, will not affect his moral attitude, which is all he is concerned about' (Striker, 1983: 162).

9. For an extended discussion, see Stephens and Feezell (2004). See also Xenakis (1969: 12–25).

10. For the early Stoics there is no 'will' as a faculty distinct from the intellect; see Kahn (1988). For Epictetus, the Stoic trains herself, through disciplined mental habituation, to accept every occurrence as it occurs.

11. According to the doctrine of providence, Zeus controls even my willing. The acts of willing I perform are thus Zeus' acts of willing since my substance is, as part of the universe, his substance too. This entails the unsavory consequence that Zeus also wills that some people be vicious. Epictetus admits that Zeus has ordained that there be both virtue and vice since a balance of opposites is needed for the harmony of the whole (1.12.16). Exactly *why* this opposition is needed for holistic harmony is not explained.

12. My translation of '... die Unabhängigkeit des Geistes von den Zuständen des Leibes verkündigt er stets ohne jegliche Einschränkung. In jeder Peristasis kann der Mensch sein Hegemonikon naturgemäss bewahren, und das Erdulden des

Schmerzes und der Krankheit ist nach Epictet ein völlig aus-
reichender sittlicher Lebenszweck' (Bonhöffer, 1894: 32).

13. Timothy Mahoney has suggested an even simpler solution: (1)
Zeus wills the rational; (2) I will the rational; therefore (3) I
will what Zeus wills.

14. Here an interesting parallel could perhaps be drawn with
Kant's idea of purposiveness without purpose in nature.

15. As we will see in Chapter 4, the world appears to the sage
quite differently than it does to us. The sage has such
discerning vision that she easily perceives the rationality of
each event. Non-Stoics can only see the randomness of events
(cf. 1.6.1–2).

16. Obviously the theological view (b) of the kind father and good
king, i.e. 'God,' is at work here.

17. Oldfather's emphasis; one wonders how Epictetus' wand
of Hermes could have transformed the Black Death, the
Holocaust, the bombings of Dresden and Hiroshima and
other large-scale atrocities of modernity.

18. For a full discussion of Epictetus' views on suicide see Bonhöffer
(1894: 23–39). For an excellent account of how the general
Stoic theory of ethics applies to the special case of suicide see
Cooper (1989).

19. Fragment 28b in Oldfather; this passage from Marcus Aurelius
iv 49. 2–6 is believed to be a direct quotation from Epictetus.

20. Cf. the motto of William the Silent: 'It is not necessary
to succeed in order to endeavor, nor to hope in order to
persevere.'

21. Inwood writes: 'On this theory, intentions are always followed
by actions unless external obstacles intervene. It is never
possible for a man to be sure that his intentions will succeed.
Since, however, we would not hold a man responsible for such
hindrances to his actions, it follows that intentions are the
correct locus of moral evaluation' (Inwood, 1985: 96). Frede
explains in greater detail the rationale behind the Stoic's
attitude toward the results of his attempted actions:

> ... the impulses of the Stoic wise man will be directed
> towards things which he, given his understanding of

the order of things, thinks are the rational things to go after. But if he does not obtain what he is impelled towards this will be a very minor loss; a loss, because other things being equal, the world would be a more reasonable place, if he did obtain what he is impelled towards given that it is not due to any failure on his part that he fails to obtain what he is after; a very minor loss, since the value of what he failed to obtain does not even begin to shift the balance if compared in weightiness to the rationality he maintained in being impelled towards the object he failed to obtain; moreover, the very fact that he did not obtain what he was after, just reveals that in this case other things were not equal, that there were overriding reasons for his lack of success, that the world is a more reasonable place because he failed. It is for this reason that he can go about things with the proverbial equanimity of a Stoic sage. For it does not really matter to him which way the things he does turn out. For, whether he succeeds or fails, it will be for the best for the world in either case. And since this is what he was aiming at in the first place when he felt impelled towards what he failed to obtain, he succeeds even in his failure. (Frede, 1986: 110)

22. De Lacy (1943: 123). To say the apparatus in the game have no intrinsic value means that their moral value is extrinsic since it relates to how we use them.

23. There is no external criterion for doing well or doing badly on the Stoic account. The Stoic accepts *whatever* results.

24. My translation of

Epictet, so ernstlich er die Wertlosigkeit der äusseren Güter für das wahre Glück betont, doch dieselben keineswegs ganz gering schätzt, sondern sich ihres Besitzes und Genusses freuen heisst, solange derselbe geboten wird. Die Apathie, die er fordert, ist, möchte ich sagen, keine psychologische, sondern nur eine moralische: wer diese äusseren Güter nicht besitzt, soll sie nicht begehren und wenn er sie verliert, nicht darüber trauern und klagen, weil hiedurch der innere Friede gestört und der sittliche Lebenszweck verfehlt wird. Wer sie aber hat, darf sich ihrer freuen und muss Gott dafür danken. Nichts ist unserem Philosophen mehr zuwider und vermag ihn mehr aufzubringen als ein unzufriedener, undankbarer Sinn, der die Gaben Gottes nicht erkennt oder gering achtet. (Bonhöffer, 1894: 41)

25. Bonhöffer is correct to note that although he has grateful appreciation for all the pleasant external things of life, Epictetus always keeps in sight the single gift of god that has unconditional value and truly makes one happy, namely, reason (Bonhöffer, 1894: 42).

26. Epictetus' position is this. Once one decides to value one's dignity as a true good and thereby chooses to measure one's interests by the standard of one's *prohairesis* rather than some other standard, then some actions become objectionable which would not be objectionable to a person using a different standard. This is what Epictetus is explaining in the following passage:

> For to one person it is reasonable to hold a chamber-pot for another, since he considers only that, if he does not hold it, he will get a beating and will not get food, whereas, if he does hold it, nothing harsh or painful will be done to him; but some other person feels that it is not merely unendurable to hold such a pot himself, but even to tolerate another's doing so. If you ask me, then, 'Shall I hold the pot or not?' I will tell you that to get food is more worthwhile (*meizona axian*) than not to get it, and to be flayed is more detrimental (*meizona apaxian*) than not to be; so that if you measure your interests by these standards, go and hold the pot. 'But it would not suit me (*all ouk an kat eme*).' That is an additional consideration, which you, and not I, must introduce into the question. For you are the one that knows yourself, how much you are worth in your own eyes and at what price you sell yourself. For different people sell themselves at different prices' (1.2.8–11).

With this passage Epictetus illustrates how one person can consider holding a chamber-pot for another as undignified and anathema to his moral character, while another can view it as quite benign and not at all harmful to his *prosōpon*; cf. also 1.2.4–7.

27. Stockdale (1978: 105).

28. For Frankl's experiences in a concentration camp see Frankl (1962). The POW Stockdale once cut his own scalp and pounded his face with a stool so that he would be disfigured and thus unsuitable for propaganda display by his captors; see Stockdale (1978).

29. Why the proper fulfillment of one's social roles is necessary to maintain one's *prohairesis* in the proper condition will be discussed at length in Chapter 4.

30. This turns on the significance of the poverty of sage-candidates like Socrates, for example.

Chapter 3

How does the Stoic love?

Other human beings, since they lie outside one's own *prohairesis*, clearly count as 'externals' just as much as inanimate objects do on Epictetus' account. Therefore, although some humans are rational, they all should be considered strictly speaking as 'indifferents' which neither contribute to one's happiness nor detract from it. Although this attitude at first glance may seem to be utterly inhuman, we shall see that on Epictetus' account of the relationship between the Stoic and his fellow-human beings, love and affection occupy a prominent position. The philanthropic[1] treatment of all people is in Epictetus, as it is in early Stoicism, a 'proper function' (*kathēkon*) of the rational being that becomes in her own interest to perform. As with inanimate objects, other people are 'materials for the volition' (1.29.2) in the sense that the individual's moral character is revealed by how she deals with them. Yet it is not initially clear what kind of content there is to the love which the Stoic shows her fellow-human beings. Are other people of any intrinsic moral value (and hence unlike inanimate objects in this respect) or do they, according to Epictetus' ethical system, in fact count only as objects toward which one is supposed to demonstrate one's social duties as if they were merely tokens in a game? As 4.7.5 suggests, it is the playing, not the tokens themselves, which matter to the Stoic. I will address this question in the course of my examination of Epictetus' account of social relationships and my interpretation of his conception of Stoic love. I will conclude this chapter by analyzing his remarkable argument that the power to love belongs only to the wise person.

A. The good of others is my own concern

The first question that we must ask about the relation of the Stoic to other persons is how it is that she comes to concern herself with them at all. Each individual acts for the sake of her own good and her own happiness, so what interest would she have in the good of others? Epictetus explains how his principle of eudaimonism rests on the nature of the human animal; Zeus has in general

> so constituted the nature of the rational animal, that he can attain nothing of his own proper goods unless he contributes something to the common interest. Hence it follows that it can no longer be regarded as unsocial to do everything for one's own sake. For what do you expect? That one should neglect oneself and his own interest? And in that case how can there be room for one and the same principle of action for all, namely, that of appropriation of their own needs?[2]

Here Epictetus adverts to the traditional Stoic concept of 'appropriation' (*oikeiōsis*), which represents the primary impulse of all living creatures.[3] He suggests that in following this natural impulse to obtain one's own private good, a human being contributes to the public good by filling her niche in the world as a whole.

Yet how can an individual's private interest ever include the interest of others? Epictetus argues in the following lengthy passage that it is a matter of how one identifies oneself.

> It is a general rule – be not deceived – that every living thing appropriates (*oikeiōtai*) nothing so much as its own interest. Whatever, then, appears to it to stand in the way of this interest, be it a brother, or father, or child, or loved one, or lover, the being hates, accuses, and curses it. For its nature is to love nothing so much as its own interest ... For this reason, if someone puts together in one scale his interest and righteousness and what is honourable and country and parents and friends, they are all safe; but if he puts his interest in one scale, and in the other friends and country and kinsmen and justice itself, all these

latter are lost because they are outweighed by his interest. For where one can say 'I' and 'mine,' to that side must the creature perforce incline; if they are in the flesh, there must the ruling power be; if they are in the volition, there must it be; if they are in externals, there must it be. If, therefore, I am where my volition is, then, and only then, will I be the friend and son and the father that I should be. For then this will be my interest – to keep my good faith, my self-respect, my forbearance, my abstinence, and my co-operation, and to maintain my relations (*tas scheseis*). (2.22.15–16 and 18–20)

So care for others becomes included in one's own private interest by deliberately identifying one's own personal good with the good of one's volition. The virtuous fulfillment of all one's familial, social, and civic roles is the demonstrative result of identifying the good with righteousness and honor. The individual judges what is good for her to be what is good for her volition. Epictetus argues that what is good for the volition will be correct judgements, i.e. the judgements in accord with its natural virtue. To value the health of the *prohairesis*, the true self, he claims, entails valuing the virtues of fidelity, self-respect, forbearance, abstinence, cooperation, etc. If, however, one locates the good anywhere other than within the virtuous norms of one's volition, then none of these virtues, nor the conduct that proceeds from them, can be in one's interest. One will of necessity not be inclined to them. I will present this argument in full and analyze it in some detail in Chapter 4.

B. Only my own conduct matters

As *Ench.* 30 indicates, one is naturally born into a relationship with a father, not a good father, with a brother perhaps, not with a good brother. One has a number of these natural relations and one also acquires other relations with friends, citizens, fellow-travellers, etc. It is incumbent upon the Stoic to fulfill her proper functions in all her natural and acquired relations. The Stoic must perform these roles virtuously if she is to act in accordance with nature and be happy. This much is clearly up to her and under her control; she is entirely free to do so. How her father and brother act toward *her*, on the other hand, is not up to her. It is completely up to *them*. Consequently, their behavior should be of no concern to her and should not interfere with her choice of actions at all. Epictetus explains that your brother's anger against you is part of *his* life, it 'is the subject matter of his own art of living, but with respect to *your* art of living it comes under the category of externals, like a farm, like health, like good repute' (1.15.1–3). A farm, one's bodily health, and the attitudes and actions of others are all equally externals, and as such the Stoic does not allow herself to be upset by them, since for her they all count as indifferents.

> 'My brother ought not to have treated me so.' No; but it is for him to look to that. As for me, no matter how he behaves, I shall observe all my relations to him as I ought. For this is my part, the other does not belong to me; in this nobody can hinder me, the other is subject to hindrance. (3.10.19–20)

The behavior of my brother is 'subject to hindrance' with respect to my own will – in other words, my will can easily be thwarted if I will that he act in a certain way. How he acts is his concern, not mine. My concern, my responsibility is only with my own conduct. The Stoic ought to 'marry,[4] get children, be active as a citizen; endure revilings, bear with an unreasonable brother, father, son, neighbour, fellow-traveller' (3.21.5), that is, she must perform her own proper functions, since they belong to her, while at the same time accepting and enduring the behavior of the people around her since that does not fall within her sphere of control. The misbehavior of others ought never to keep her from fulfilling her own proper functions.

Epictetus tries to convince the person who insists on complaining about the misbehavior of others with the following reasoning:

> For, look you, can we escape from human beings? And how is it possible? But can we, if they associate with us, change them? And who vouchsafes us that power? What alternative remains, then,

or what method can we find for living with them? Some such method as that, while they will act as seems best to them, we shall none the less be in a state conformable to nature. (1.12.18–19)

It is simply not in our power to transform people into virtuous, cooperative folk. They will ultimately act as seems best to them regardless of how we think they ought to act. We control our own disposition, but not theirs. We can try to effect their uncivil behavior by appealing to their reason, but if they are refractory, then we can only patiently endure their conduct without allowing it, no matter how bad we think it is, to dislodge us from our own virtuous, serene state of character. As we saw in Chapter 2 the Stoic attitude is that we must make the best of what is up to us (in this case, our own conduct) and calmly accept the rest (the behavior of others) as it is.

If it so happens that our parents are not of a pleasant kind, then that should not be something we get upset about and resent, because again that too is not in our control, not something in our power to choose. So when Epictetus' interlocutor complains about his parents, Epictetus asks:

Well, was it permitted you to step forward and make selection, saying, 'Let such-and-such man have intercourse with such-and-such woman at this hour, that I may be born'? It was not permitted you; but your parents had to exist first, then you had to be born as you were born. Of what kind of parents? Of such as they were. (1.12.28–9)

Nature permits us neither to choose our parents nor to trade them away once we have them. Whatever their temperaments are, they are our parents, and so as our parents we must fulfill our proper functions toward them by being obedient, tolerant, and helpful.

Since the nature of things is such that only our own decisions and actions are up to us, we are accordingly only accountable for how we choose to deal with the things under our control.

As for parents, the gods have released you from accountability; as for brothers, they have released you; as for body, they have released you; and for property, death, life. Well, for what have they made you accountable? For the only thing that is under your control – the proper use of impressions. (1.12.33–4)

How we judge the sense-impressions we receive, and then how we choose to act and react, are the only things for which we are accountable. That is why Epictetus says that nothing is disgraceful to you that is not your own doing; hence the poverty of your parents, the character of your father, a headache, a fever, all such things are not disgraceful to you because you are not responsible for them (3.26.8–10). External conditions beyond your power to effect need not be a source of disgrace for you.

Now the wording in 2.22.18, where our philosopher instructs us to put our country and parents and friends in the same scale as our interest in order to keep them all safe, would seem to imply that we are actually including the people themselves and the country itself among our own goods. Yet this is not what Epictetus means, since for him all these things are externals and so must be considered indifferents. Rather, Epictetus maintains that the right *prohairesis* is the righteous, honorable, noble, and just one. As we will see in Chapter 4, this is so because the virtues, not the vices, are what are good for us, i.e. conducive to our mental health given the nature of human beings. The Stoic values as goods not her parents, siblings, and country, but rather the aforementioned virtues, and these virtues in turn make for the preservation of all our relationships. Thus the virtuous treatment of our parents, siblings, children, friends, fellow-citizens, fellow-travellers, etc. only derives indirectly from our decision to value the virtues necessary for maintaining our volition in its proper, healthy state in accord with nature. Hence, on this analysis, the beneficent, faithful, philanthropic behavior which we manifest in our relations with the people in our lives is in fact motivated not externally by concern for the people themselves. Rather, the philanthropic behavior we show others is motivated completely internally by concern for our own *psuchē* and its healthy (virtuous) condition. The proper conduct *toward* other people therefore counts as a good to the Stoic, since it derives from and is required by the virtues of the self. People *themselves*, however,

do not count as 'goods' (*agatha*) though of all externals they are
the most 'worthwhile' (*axia*).

This account may seem to preclude true altruism. Yet we must
remember here that for Epictetus there is only one principle of
action for all beings, namely, appropriation (*oikeiōsis*) to its own
needs, i.e. each being does everything for its own sake. This is
simply the way nature is. Yet, as we saw, this does not at all eliminate
the rationality of acts of unselfish love aimed at the benefit of
others. Bonhöffer explains how this is possible.

> It is clear that the duty of unselfish love can only then exist
> together with eudaimonism when the love is recognized as an
> essential quality of the mental itself, so that the practice of love
> appears only as a piece of mental self-preservation. Now Epictetus
> expresses this just as clearly as possible by sharply distinguishing
> eudaimonism from egoism (*philauton*), subsuming the altruistic
> duties under the duties that are in the higher sense egoistic, and
> laying down the proposition: God has established the nature of
> the rational being so that it can obtain no good peculiar to itself
> if it is not at the same time of public utility. (1.19.13)[5]

The Stoic who risks her own life to rescue her drowning child,
therefore, does so not because her child's life is a good that demands
her protection, but because the protection of one's child is one of the
proper functions of a parent, and the performance of one's proper
functions is necessary for preserving the right condition of one's
volition and being happy (*eudaimōn*). Thus she seeks and achieves
her own good in performing her proper function (protecting her
child) and, because of the nature of things, in doing so she also
secures the good of another (the child's welfare).

The situation the Stoic is in, relative to material possessions and
the public good, is nevertheless a complex one. Now clearly when
it comes to contending for externals the Stoic does not hesitate
to yield them to others. He happily relinquishes externals to his
relatives since, first of all, this allows him to preserve the proper
non-combative relationships with them and thereby maintain the
right (virtuous) state of his volition for his own sake. But

... furthermore, he who gives up some of the externals achieves the good. 'My father is taking away my money.' But he is doing you no harm. 'My brother is going to get the larger part of the farm.' Let him have all he wants. That does not help him at all to get a part of your modesty, does it, or of your fidelity, or of your brotherly love (*philadelphou*)? (3.3.8–9; cf. also 2.10.8–9)

In ceding material wealth to others the Stoic is not giving up any true goods at all, but rather she actually gains the true goods of modesty, fidelity, and love of siblings for herself. She values internals, her own virtues of character, so she gladly leaves farm, property, money, and all such externals to others, not because her aim is to benefit them, but because she considers material possessions to be indifferents with no intrinsic (moral) value at all.

Since the Stoic does not regard material wealth as a good, she of course does not exert herself to acquire it, but rather concentrates on keeping her true self in a virtuous state in accordance with nature. Yet to keep her *prohairesis* in this moral condition she must also perform all her social, familial, and civic roles, which include exercising her benevolence and philanthropy. The difficult question raised then is: what form does this benevolence and philanthropy take? If the Stoic is to confer true goods upon her fellow-human beings, then improving their economic situation and material living conditions would not be an appropriate strategy, since she believes the good to lie in internals, not in external earthly putative 'goods.'

Now as we saw in 3.3.8–9, the Stoic happily forgoes earthly 'goods' to those who want them from her. In this case her philanthropy manifests itself in not fighting people for these earthly 'goods,' but in passively allowing them to get what they desire while maintaining her equanimity toward them. But does this entail that the Stoic be generally prodigal? How does she demonstrate her philanthropy toward those in abject poverty who are in desperate need of food, clothing, and shelter if she does not herself have an abundance of such things?

A wealthy Stoic could contend that she has obligations to her children, e.g. to be wealthy enough to give them a good education.

If she is a businesswoman, the Stoic's career role would make financial prosperity an obligation in itself. This is the sort of justification Seneca must have given for lending his money at usurious rates in amassing his fortune. But to limit the beneficiaries of one's material wealth to one's family members alone would be to neglect one's role as a *kosmopolitēs*, a citizen of the *universe*.

The financial responsibilities of an emperor like Marcus Aurelius could provide an easy rationalization for considering adding tax moneys to the state coffers a 'duty.' But his role as emperor includes providing for the welfare of everyone in the entire empire. If he privately owned a large warehouse of food and clothing and the hungry homeless of Rome came to him begging for access to his warm, dry building and its stores of food, wouldn't he be generous to his fellow-citizens and subjects? As for a private citizen, if needy panhandlers asked her for money, the charitable Stoic would be able to spare a fair portion of the money she had on her.

These are cases of quite passive charity on the part of the Stoic, and they also assume she has the material 'goods' to give. But what if, like Socrates and Diogenes, the Stoic simply does not have a great deal of material wealth to give away? How eagerly will the Stoic endeavor to gain material wealth to donate to others when she does not even consider putative earthly 'goods' to be real goods at all? Bonhöffer's judgement is, I think, a fair one when he writes that positive, active concern for the welfare of others is much less conspicuous in Epictetus than passive charity: 'The impulse to energetic, dedicated work for the elimination of human misery is necessarily weakened by the exaggerated contempt of all earthly goods of happiness.'[6]

The Stoic has no drive to amass material wealth, because for her true wealth is not to be found in the external world in material 'goods.' Rather, it lies in a virtuous state of character, in mental serenity, and in the wisdom of correct judgements. The Stoic is rich in *autarkeia*. That is why, when it comes to externals, she needs no more than the barest material necessities of life. She is not niggardly with the material wealth she does happen to have, on the one hand; yet she refuses to sacrifice her own true goods, that is, her moral integrity, in order to procure so-called material 'goods' for others (see *Ench.*

24.3), on the other. The difficult question, however, lies in the wide area of ground between these two limits. How actively must the Stoic work for the economic and material improvement of all her fellow-human beings in order to perform her proper function as a citizen of the universe? Might this beneficent activity for the public welfare conflict with the Stoic vigorously working to provide for the private material needs of her family, as a good parent should?

In answer to the first question, Bonhöffer believes that the Stoics' idealistic disregard of all external goods hindered them from

> ... showing a real interest in the economic and cultural problems of the community. With all that however it must be admitted that they, perhaps even with a certain inconsistency, zealously defended the value of patriotism and the duty of work for public utility and in case they held a public office, they made it their duty to take care of the general welfare with all faithfulness and conscientiousness.[7]

So the answer to the first question seems to be that the Stoic works for the economic welfare of her community conscientiously in her role as a public official to the extent that it is required of her. As for the second question, we should similarly suppose she earns a living to provide financial support for her family in her role as a parent to the extent that her family needs adequate food, clothing, and shelter (yet here austerity and harsh practicality is no doubt the rule for Musonius Rufus and Epictetus). Yet, for Epictetus, the Stoic does not primarily toil to garner material wealth to donate as humanitarian aid to others, but rather she can try to improve the lives of others instead through the manifestation of her moral excellence. 'Whoever cannot serve his native country by the holding of offices or by financial sacrifice may do it in this way, that by his word and example he acts upon improving his fellow-citizens: in this way he is of more use to it than if he constructed stoas and baths' (*Ench.* 24.4).[8] This is much more characteristic of how the Stoic manifests her benevolence, because she is attempting to confer true goods upon her fellow-citizens by urging them to gain the right judgements and virtues of character that will produce mental freedom and true happiness. Epictetus cites the examples of faith-fully nursing one's sick daughter (1.11) and bravely accompanying one's son on a dangerous sea voyage (3.7.3) as deeds of love which require no material wealth to assist others. We will return at the end of this chapter to discuss the means of helping others that is most in keeping with the spirit of Epictetus' Stoicism.

Finally, a point of clarification is needed. The Stoic acts for the sake of another, e.g. her son's welfare, *because* it is his welfare. This is typically thought of as acting *for his sake*. But again the Stoic has a self-regarding motive for so acting: she wants to be virtuous for *her own* sake. It probably strikes us as very odd to view the performance of the roles and the execution of the proper familial, civic, social, and global humanitarian functions as goods, but not to view the people who are the beneficiaries of these deeds as goods. Yet Epictetus must maintain this in order to keep the Stoic's happiness always within her power to preserve. A question that arises from this position, however, is that if the very lives of other people do not even count as goods for the Stoic, then how can she be properly said to love others at all? To answer this question we must next turn to Epictetus' account of natural human affection.

C. Human affection and feeling

Epictetus believes that loving concern for others is inherent in (non-pathological cases of) human nature. He asserts that humans are by nature noble, have a sense of shame, and that it is our nature to subordinate pleasure to the virtuous performance of our social duties. Benevolent impulses, according to him, naturally override our desire for pleasure

> ... in the case of the human being (*anthrōpos*), it is not his material substance that we should honour, his bits of flesh, but the principal things (*ta proēgoumena*). What are these? The duties of citizenship, marriage, begetting children, reverence to god, care for parents, in a word, desire, avoidance, choice, refusal, the proper performance of each one of these acts, and that is, in

accordance with our nature. And what is our nature? To act as free people (*eleutheroi*), as noble, as self-respecting. Why, what other living being blushes, what other comprehends the impression of shame? And it is our nature to subordinate pleasure to these duties as their servant, their minister, so as to arouse our interest and keep us acting in accordance with nature. (3.7.25–8)

Here Epictetus infers from the empirical observation that only human beings blush and feel shame that our nature as human beings is to esteem the noble, respectable performance of all our human roles as citizens, spouses, parents, worshippers of god, children, etc. Because of our instinctive response to feel shame and blush when we know that we are acting disgracefully, he argues that respectable, virtuous action arises quite normally from our basic human nature. Thus he even asserts that it is in accordance with our human nature to subordinate pleasure to the proper performance of our social roles.[9] Therefore, Epictetus reminds us that when abroad, the intention of the traveller who is just passing through is not to stay permanently at a nice inn and selfishly indulge in the amenities of a temporary lodging, but rather

… your plan (*prothesis*) is the other thing, to return to your country, to relieve the fear of your kinsmen, to do the duties of a citizen yourself, to marry, bring up children, hold the customary offices. For you did not come into the world to select unusually fine places, I expect, but to live and go about your business in the place where you were born and were enrolled as a citizen. (2.23.38–9)

He asserts we are by nature born communitarian (*phusei koinōnikoi gegonamen*) (2.20.13). Furthermore, since we do in fact have this natural fellowship (*koinōnia*), he urges that we ought by all means to guard it (2.20.8). In support of this assertion he cites the inconsistency of Epicurus' actions. Epicurus denies that there is a natural fellowship among rational beings on the one hand, yet he exerts much effort writing books and trying to persuade people that he is right on the other hand (2.20.6–14). But if he believes what he says, why should he worry about people being deceived about this matter and why would he bother to take pains on their account to try to set them straight? Now it *may* simply be a personal quirk that doing philosophy happens to give Epicurus pleasure.[10] Yet Epictetus thinks Epicurus' actions in fact reveal his true (philanthropic) sentiment, claiming that he becomes the advocate to denounce his own doctrines (2.20.16). So, were the Stoic to say that we should find satisfaction in doing the deeds required by our mutual relations, we could construe this 'should' both descriptively and normatively – descriptively, since it is both natural and normal for us to feel satisfaction in performing our proper social functions, and normatively since it is good, healthy, and thus rational for us to do so.

Elsewhere Epictetus claims the nature of human beings is 'gentle, and affectionate, and faithful' (4.1.126), and so he infers that family affection (*to philostorgon*) is in accordance with nature and good (*kalon*) and is compatible with what is reasonable (*to eulogiston*) (1.11.17–19). Moreover, he not only says that affection for our own children is a natural sentiment (1.23.3), but he even asserts 'once a child is born, it is no longer up to us not to love (*stergein*) it or to care for it' (1.23.5).

Now this last assertion is very significant for Epictetus, since he is using his emblematic phrase 'not up to us.' Epictetus may mean that after a certain time, having bonded with the child, it is simply impossible for the normal parent not to be strongly and permanently positively disposed toward her child. An alternative interpretation is that 'what we have at birth is instincts; this instinct does not come into play until we actually have offspring, but when we do, we do not have to learn to love them.'[11] On this view, the Stoic's innate nature moves her to bond with and care for her own offspring. Moreover, this motivation is reaffirmed by her judgement (the recognition of her duty) to so act. She acts on her rational decision *and* in accord with her natural inclination. This nurturant love for her child is so strong that the normal parent is incapable of suppressing it even if she wanted to.

The Stoic cannot feel indifferent about her child, because it is not possible for a human being absolutely to lose the affections of a human being (*tas kinēseis tas anthrōpikas*) (2.20.19). On Epictetus' conception of human psychology, the child abuser would be a pathological aberration of nature. The mother who beats her child would be acting contrary to (her maternal) nature, on the Stoic account.

Epictetus holds not only that we are by nature social beings (1.23.1), but that we have a natural sense of self-respect, fidelity, affection, helpfulness, and of keeping our hands off one another (2.10.22–3). He sees all of these as natural human sentiments, but he also believes that Stoicism works to strengthen them since upon completing their Stoic education people ought to be 'ready to help one another' (3.21.9). Consequently, beneficent conduct toward one's fellows is both in the Stoic's self-interest (since it is required by the virtues needed for a sound *prohairesis*) and so rational to choose, and it normally stems directly from our human nature.

Epictetus reasons as follows. A thing is faring badly when it acts contrary to its own nature. What then is the nature of human beings? 'To bite, and kick, and throw into prison, and behead? No, but to do good, to work together, and to pray for the success of others. Therefore, he is faring badly, whether you will or no, when he acts unfeelingly' (4.1.121–2). Epictetus' optimistic view is that animosity and hostility are contrary to human nature. To act belligerently toward other people is to act contrary to one's own human nature and thus to fare badly. But the Stoic acts according to human nature not just in refraining from harming others, but also in caring about and feeling for them. Epictetus argues that the Stoic is not, therefore, nor ought he to be utterly impassive, since it would be contrary to his nature as a human being, 'for I ought not to be unfeeling (*apathē*) like a statue, but should maintain my relations, both natural and acquired, as a pious person, as son, as brother, as father, as citizen' (3.2.4).

The picture of the Stoic's attitude toward others that has emerged is this. Since she defines her own good as one and the same as the noble, the honorable, and the just, the preservation of her natural and acquired relations becomes necessary for keeping her volition in a healthy state, i.e. in a state in accord with nature's norm. Thus virtuous conduct toward others is required for her own intellectual self-preservation and *eudaimonia*. Moreover, that she is not a statue since she is also instinctively affectionate, gentle, faithful, helpful, and loving, and so is drawn to fulfill all her social, familial, and civic roles is a sign of what is natural, i.e. healthy and normal. Nonetheless, she must not let her feelings for others disrupt her mental serenity, for

> ... the work of philosophy is ... that each person passes his life to himself, free from pain, fear, and perturbation, at the same time maintaining with his associates both the natural and acquired relationships, those namely of son, father, brother, citizen, husband, wife, neighbour, fellow-traveller, ruler, and subject. (2.14.8)

But how can the Stoic maintain her relationships with other people without being unfeeling, and yet without becoming upset when those she loves suffer or are lost? It is not up to her not to love her children; yet how can she love them without also feeling pain when they are hurt?

In order to resolve this dilemma we must first distinguish between the natural feelings that the Stoic has (affection, gentleness, helpfulness, etc.) that are entirely positive, and the feelings that disrupt her mental serenity. From the Stoic's perspective, when one's child dies, grief is not natural in the sense of appropriate, it is natural in the sense of typical, that is, typical of non-Stoics. Epictetus has said that family affection (*to philostorgon*) and fondness (*sterktikon*) are natural human feelings, and so Epictetus does not consider them to be 'passions' (*pathē*). The Stoic is not supposed to be devoid of these natural, positive feelings, which Epictetus evidently would include among the classic *eupatheiai* of orthodox Stoicism, namely joy/delight (*chara*), caution (*eulabeia*) and wishing (*boulēsis*); the Stoic is devoid only of the overly intense emotions or passions which destroy her *ataraxia, euroia,* and *apatheia*.[12] We could say, then, that the Stoic is passionless but not unfeeling.

Epictetus holds that only (Stoic) philosophy in fact can produce in us peace from *erōs* (sexual passion), sorrow, envy, and other passions (3.13.10). Thus, as Bonhöffer correctly observes, Epictetus agrees with the early Stoa in rejecting the sexual *erōs* as pathos: '*Erōs* is therefore here interpreted as an emotion disturbing inner peace and true happiness.'[13]

A short digression on the *eupatheiai* may be instructive here. The *eupatheiai* are importantly but subtly different than the disturbing *pathē*. For example, the Stoic experiences *chara* about her choices. She is delighted about her proper functioning, but generally her functioning is toward an external. Thus it will be directed toward having successfully achieved some external. The lover, for example, delights in the success of her loved one by virtue of being related to him. Consequently, the familiarization with one's beloved is the source of one's *chara*.

As we have already seen (in Chapter 2, section A and elsewhere), Epictetus often stresses the importance of maintaining caution (*eulabeia*) and carefulness (*epimeleia*) in dealing with *phantasiai*. Caution and carefulness manifest reasonable concern, in contrast to the irrational *pathē* of worry and nervousness.

The third 'good-feeling' is *boulēsis*. This is the (rational) wanting of something as good. It is a desire for the continuation and expression of one's internal (virtuous) states, and that entails desires for externals because it is in this secondary desire that the primary desire of *boulēsis* consists. The hungry Stoic is wanting (*boulēsis*) her own wanting (*hormē* as *kathēkon*) of food. The primary object of her wanting is thus her perfect way of wanting. The secondary object of her wanting is the food. The pleasant sensations of eating the food are not the same as the delight in those sensations. The latter constitutes a *pathos* for the Stoics, though the former, the titillation of the palate, does not.

Now to return to the question at hand: how does the Stoic love others in a way that does not leave her open to emotional distress and inner disquietude? In other words, how does the Stoic love others without letting her love become a *pathos*?

D. Stoic love is free and painless

Part of maintaining one's natural and acquired relations involves easing the pain of others by providing emotional support and comfort. Often enough our family members or friends are troubled, mourn, or grieve, and it would be callously unfeeling of us to ignore their distress. But what is the Stoic supposed to do, for example, when her mother misses her?

> But my mother mourns because she does not see me. – Yes, but why did she not learn the meaning of these words of the philosophers? And I am not saying that you ought to take no pains to keep her from lamenting, but only that a person ought not to want at all costs what is not his own. Now another's grief is no concern of mine, but my own grief is. Therefore, I will put an end at all costs to what is my own concern, for it is under my control: and that which is another's concern I will endeavour to check to the best of my ability, but my effort to do so will not be made at all costs. Otherwise I shall be fighting against god, I shall be setting myself in opposition to Zeus, I shall be arraying myself against him in regard to his administration of the universe. (3.24.22–4)

Since the lamenting of my mother is an external and is not under my control, I should try my best to ease her pain and comfort her (since this much I can attempt and is required of me as her son); yet I should not want her to stop grieving at all costs because this is not under my control. My mother's grief is her own concern, not mine, because it is the result of her own judgements about external events. If I wish to have the power to end her suffering, then I am wishing for the nature of the universe to be different than it is. I would be wishing to control my own judgements and hers as well, but this is simply not how Zeus has established the nature of things. I can and certainly should attempt to relieve her distress since the *attempt* is up to me. Yet the result of my attempt at consoling her lies beyond my *prohairesis* and so is properly speaking not my concern. If I am to be a rational Stoic, then I must not sacrifice my own mental serenity to my desire to end my mother's grief. Ultimately she will determine whether she can bear her troubles or whether she will continue to feel grief. Her grief, then, is up to her, not me.

Here the external behavior of the Stoic who endeavors to comfort someone who is in sorrow appears to be identical to the non-Stoic who not only tries to relieve another's sorrow but also shares in it. The crucial difference between the Stoic and the non-Stoic in this case is not that the non-Stoic is sincere in wanting the griever's sorrow to end whereas the Stoic is not really sincere. They both truly want the other person's suffering to cease, but the difference is that the Stoic wants it to cease *if Zeus so wills*, and she does not 'want it at all costs,' i.e. she doesn't sacrifice her own imperturbability in the consoling, while the non-Stoic does take on and share in the sorrow of the other person.

> When you see someone weeping in sorrow, either because a child has gone on a journey, or because he has lost his property, beware that the impression (*phantasia*) not carry you away that he is in the midst of external ills, but keep directly before you this thought: 'It is not what has happened that distresses this person (for it does not distress another), but his judgement about it.' Do not, however, hesitate to sympathize with him so far as words go, and, if occasion arises, even to groan with him; but be careful not to groan also internally. (*Ench.* 16)

The Stoic may be in a situation in which by vocally groaning with the griever she may help ease the other's pain. In doing so the Stoic demonstrates that she cares about the griever and is trying to help him. The natural affection she has for the fellow manifests itself in this external behavior. Yet the Stoic must also remind herself not to let the griever's distress drag her down into the same state. The Stoic is thus careful not to groan internally, i.e. not to allow the *pathos* of the other person to take hold of her own inner self. The Stoic, we could say, *shows* sympathy to the unfortunate wretch who, because he incorrectly judges some happening evil, makes himself sorrowful, but the Stoic does not *feel* sympathy for him because this would be to subject her own soul to a *pathos* on account of the mistaken judgement of another.[14] So the Stoic empathizes by means of her words of comfort and external behavior while not making the mistake of succumbing to the pathological state of another by allowing herself to suffer internally.

On Epictetus' account, consequently, one should rejoice with others and share in their happiness, but not share in their misery. Misery comes from misjudging an external to be evil.

> Let not that which in the case of another is contrary to nature become an evil for you; for you are born not to be humiliated along with others, nor to share in their misfortune, but to share in their good fortune. If, however, someone is unfortunate, remember that his misfortune concerns himself. (3.24.1–2)

(See Chapter 2, section B for a discussion of Epictetus' idea of good fortune.) Here again Epictetus' account is wholly optimistic in its teleology. He says 'it is not becoming for us to be unhappy on any person's account, but to be happy because of all, and above all others because of the god who has made us for this end' (3.24.63). Each person's misfortune and unhappiness is self-imposed, on Epictetus' view; they result from making wrong judgements about things, namely, judgements contrary to nature. Thus no matter how much another person suffers because of what she perceives to be a catastrophic evil, it is simply not becoming, i.e. it does not fit our human nature, for us to be miserable on someone else's account. Epictetus insists that one ought to share exclusively in the positive feelings of others.

Epictetus reasons that since, for example, 'it is impossible for one human being always to live with another' (3.24.20), it is foolish and slavish to wish never to be separated from a loved one and to weep and lament when one is so separated. It is to forget how things are and irrationally to wish for the impossible. 'Yes, but I want my little children and my wife to be with me. – Are they yours? Do they not belong to him who gave them? To him who made you? Will you not, therefore, give up what is not your own?' (4.1.107). Everything extra-prohairetic belongs to Zeus, since he is the one who gives and takes them away in exercising his control over them.

But only prohairetic things truly belong to the individual, so one is entitled to lay claim only to them.

Even a person's own family members should not be claimed as one's own possessions because, since god controls the external circumstances of life, each person's life does not really belong to anyone but god. For this reason Epictetus believes one should not speak of losing something which one never truly *owned* in the first place. 'Never say about anything, "I have lost it," but only "I have given it back." Is your child dead? It has been given back. Is your wife dead? She has been given back' (*Ench.* 11). One's loved ones are not part of one's self; they lie outside one's *prohairesis*. Like all externals, then, they should be enjoyed if and as long as one has them, yet they should be taken care of as things that are not one's own, like travellers treat their inn. 'And if you wish by all means your children to live, or your wife, or your brother, or your friends, is it up to you? – No, nor those either' (4.1.67). To remember that the lives of others are not up to you should suffice to prevent the sensible person from desperately wishing them to live no matter what. 'If you wish for your children and your wife and your friends to live for ever, you are silly; for you are wishing that things not up to you should be up to you, and things not yours should be yours' (*Ench.* 14). The death of every person is inevitable because Zeus has made death the natural end to life. To wish that one's loved ones were immune from death is ridiculous, because it is to wish that mortals were immortal.

> Yes, but what if my friends over there die? – Why, what else than that mortals died? Or how can you wish to reach old age yourself, and at the same time not behold the death of any that you love? Do you not know that in the long course of time many different things by necessity happen ... (3.24.27–8)

Death ought not to be the cause of misery because it is a necessary part of the natural course of events. Therefore, the death of a loved one should not be a disturbing surprise or a cause of alarm.

But if the Stoic really loves her husband, children, and friends, then how can she *help* but be distressed when they die? After all, the death of a loved one is not merely the death of a mortal. It is the permanent end of an irreplaceable person who is the object of one's adoration. Doesn't loving such a person necessarily entail always wanting him to live and be well, and consequently being greatly upset when he does not? Once again Epictetus insists that the proper Stoic attitude must be unilaterally positive: to enjoy those who are with us while they are with us, but not to grieve when they are gone. Quite prosaically he states that the nature of the universe is such that 'some must remain with each other, while others must depart, and that though we must rejoice in those who dwell with us, yet we must not grieve at those who depart' (3.24.11). The object of the Stoic's love should be enjoyed as long as it is present. Its absence should not be allowed to convert that joy into sadness. The Stoic is supposed to rejoice in the associates that Zeus has seen fit to give her for the period of time he determines. Yet when those people depart, as they eventually must, for the Stoic then to feel bitter would be contrary to her nature as a rational being, according to Epictetus, because it would be to fail to recognize and accept the nature of things.

The way the Stoic prevents herself from being saddened and distressed by the absence of something or someone she loves is constantly to remind herself of the impermanent, transitory nature of every external to which she would attach herself. In this way Epictetus seems to think the Stoic will not allow that attachment to become a chain which would eventually drag her down into misery and grief when the object of the attachment departs or is destroyed.

> Whenever you grow attached to something, do not act as though it were one of those things that cannot be taken away, but as though it were something like a jar or a crystal goblet, so that when it breaks you will remember what it was like, and not be troubled. So too in life; if you kiss your child, your brother, your friend, never allow your fancy free rein, nor your exuberant spirits to go as far as they like, but hold them back, stop them, just like those who stand behind generals when they ride in triumph, and keep reminding them that they are mortal. In such fashion

you too remind yourself that the object of your love is mortal; it is not one of your own possessions; it has been given you for the present, not inseparably nor forever, but like a fig, or a cluster of grapes, at a fixed season of the year, and that if you hanker for it in the winter, you are a fool. If in this way you long for your son, or your friend, at a time when he is not given to you, rest assured that you are hankering for a fig in winter. For as winter is to a fig, so is every state of affairs, which arises out of the universe, in relation to the things which are destroyed in accordance with that same state of affairs. (3.24.84–7; cf. *Ench.* 3)

Epictetus believes that if one remembers the fragility of the things one loves, one can then restrain one's natural affection and stop the feeling of love from intensifying into an uncontrollable, damaging *pathos*. The rational considerations of the temporariness of the liaison, the inevitable separations from the loved one, and his eventual death function to prevent the Stoic from being overpowered by her emotions and foolishly desiring her loved one 'out of season.' If the Stoic has the mental strength and discipline to 'hold back her exuberant spirits' short of building into a *pathos*, then she will safeguard herself from the frustration and misery of wanting grapes in winter or wishing her deceased husband were still with her. For Epictetus these two desires are equally irrational, equally avoidable, and it seems qualitatively, if not quantitatively, the same.

The goal of Stoic philosophy here is consequently to be able to control one's emotions so that they never subject the Stoic to painful, disturbing feelings that rob her of her mental quietude and inner harmony. If she is successful at keeping her natural feelings from being a source of perturbation and distress, then her mental freedom and serenity will be ensured. Clearly Epictetus regards all emotional pain and mental disharmony as things to be avoided at all costs. By 'reining in' her fancy and stopping her enjoyment of an external from becoming a *pathos* that would destroy her serenity, the Stoic can both preserve her *ataraxia* and allow herself to derive some small, safe amount of pleasure from that external. This safe amount of pleasure, however, does not of course add to the Stoic's happiness, since to grant this would be to capitulate to Epicureanism.

Epictetus recommends the following method for mitigating one's pleasure in externals so that one does not come to depend upon them for one's happiness:

> Furthermore, at the very moment when you are taking delight in something, call to mind the opposite impressions. What harm is there if you whisper to yourself, at the very moment you are kissing your child, and say, 'Tomorrow you will die'? So likewise to your friend, 'Tomorrow you will go abroad, or I shall, and we shall never see each other again'? (3.24.88)

One might object that the harm that lies in calling to mind the potential loss of the object of one's love every time one is currently enjoying it is that one is precisely robbing oneself of the full enjoyment of that loved one, that one is spoiling the sweetest, richest, and most pleasant feeling of love for another by reminding oneself of the precariousness of having the loved one around. But even if greater gratification were afforded by this unchecked absorption in an external, the Stoic would consider such enhanced present pleasure not to be worth the future anguish resulting from the inevitable absence of the external that will accompany that pleasure. By not soberly reminding oneself that one's loved one may at any moment leave, one is recklessly indulging in the external with such emotional abandon that one is unnecessarily risking the security of one's happiness. One is inviting the mental pain that will result from separation from the external to which one has imprudently allowed oneself to become deeply, and so dangerously, attached.

By preparing herself to live on unperturbedly when the object of her love is gone, on the other hand, the Stoic effectively (supposedly?) insulates herself from any future emotional distress. She does not count on any externals, even her dearest family members, for her own happiness.

> This is what you ought to practise from morning till evening. Begin with the most trifling things, the ones most exposed to

injury, like a pot, or a cup, and then advance to a tunic, a paltry
dog, a mere horse, a bit of land; then to yourself, your body,
and its members, your children, wife, brothers. Look about on
every side and cast these things away from you. Purify your judgements, for fear lest something of what is not your own may be
fastened to them, or grown together with them, and may give
you pain when it is torn loose. (4.1.111–12)

Epictetus does not mean that one should literally cast away all these
externals from oneself. Rather, he is describing the rational self-
training or self-therapy (what he calls *askēsis* at 3.24.84 etc.) that
will prepare him to remain steadfast in the face of the inevitable
so-called 'misfortunes' of life. He simply means that one should
not mistakenly make a habit of fastening one's desire too firmly to
externals by judging that one needs them to be happy.

The following objection to the Stoic attitude toward other people
may be raised at this point. In insulating herself from the loss of
loved ones by reminding herself of their mortality and stopping her
emotional attachment to them from becoming something upon
which her happiness depends, doesn't the Stoic thereby emotionally
isolate herself from everyone? The answer to this objection seems
to me to be a definite 'yes.' Yet this is not to grant that there is a
grievous flaw in Epictetus' conception of the Stoic attitude toward
other people. There is no shortcoming in the external behavior
of the Stoic since, as we have seen throughout this chapter, the
Stoic conscientiously performs all of her social, familial, and civic
functions. It is just that the Stoic refuses to subject her happiness
to any external contingency. Hence with respect to her inner state,
her emotional isolation from others is simply a concomitant of her
autarkeia (self-sufficiency), but it does not by any means lead to the
neglect or abandonment of the people for whom the Stoic feels
natural affection. As evidence of this I need only cite the passage
where Epictetus states that it may become 'necessary for me to risk
my life for my friend,' or it may become 'my duty (*kathēkon*) even
to die for him' (2.7.3). So the Stoic may indeed be in a situation in
which she would be compelled to risk her own life for another, but
we must remember that her life is simply an external, and so while

it itself is of no intrinsic value, the use which she makes of it does matter, since that pertains to the morality of her character. Thus to preserve her virtuous character she may be required to sacrifice her life for a friend; yet she will endeavor to keep her mental serenity intact no matter what happens to her or to others.

A second difficulty can be couched in these terms. In making herself invulnerable to emotional pain doesn't the Stoic also make herself incapable of genuine, heartfelt human compassion for others? Here we must be clear about our understanding of 'compassion.' In so far as this is an inner feeling of pity that the commiserator has for the sufferer the Stoic does indeed experience it; she does feel sorry for the person suffering, not because she believes the sufferer to be burdened by real evils, but because the sufferer is enslaved by her own mistaken judgement that her current woes derive from external things and not from her own judgement about those things. Bonhöffer explains this well in his comments on *Ench.* 16:

> The Stoic who sighs with someone need not therefore also renounce his correct conception; rather he will do everything in order to soothe the one suffering and to encourage him to steadfastness. Where this is not possible, he will show his philanthropy in this way, that he puts himself at least seemingly in the standpoint of the one suffering. Moreover, the Stoic will indeed feel with the sufferer a certain regret, less on account of his external suffering than on account of his internal weakness and blindness. This rational regret, that is so to speak only intellectual, not emotional, is often expressed by Epictetus.[15]

So once again we can say that the Stoic acts with compassion by trying to remove the misery of the sufferer. Yet in making this attempt she will not allow herself to be ensnared by the sufferer's *pathos*. That is, the Stoic is careful to stop short of feeling the pathological sorrow of the sufferer and thus internally being disturbed like the sufferer. Stoic compassion, therefore, consists of the rational regret or pity Bonhöffer describes coupled with a sincere urge to help the person in sorrow.

We now have a fairly complete picture of the nature of Stoic affection and the way the Stoic loves others according to Epictetus. The Stoic loves other people in a very free, giving way. Her love is not at all conditional upon its being reciprocated by the person loved. The Stoic does not compromise her own moral integrity or mental serenity in her love of others, nor is it precluded by knowledge of the mortality of her loved ones. Rather, the Stoic's love and natural affection is tempered by reason, and it serves only to enrich her humanity, never to subject her to emotional or mental torment.

> How, then, shall I become affectionate (*philostorgos*)? – As one of noble spirit, as one who is fortunate; for it is against all reason to be abject, or broken in spirit, or to depend on something other than yourself, or even to blame either god or human. I would have you become affectionate in such a way as to maintain at the same time all these rules; if, however, by virtue of this natural affection, whatever it is you call by that name, you are going to be a slave and miserable, it does not profit you to be affectionate. And what keeps you from loving a person as one subject to death, as one who may leave you? Did not Socrates love his own children? But in a free spirit, as one who remembers that it was his first duty to be a friend to the gods. (3.24.58–60)

The Stoic loves freely in the sense that she does not allow her love to enslave her happiness. In other words, she does not permit her love of others to become such that her happiness depends upon always having these loved ones with her. This is because the Stoic does not allow her love ever to be a cause of loneliness, bitterness, or misery.

The kind of love which involves sacrificing one's freedom of will and dignity, in order to appease demands made by one's lover, Epictetus considers to be a terrible form of emotional servitude.

> Were you never in love with anyone, a pretty girl, or pretty boy, a slave, a freedman? – What, then, has that to do with being either a slave or free? – Were you never commanded by your

sweetheart to do something you didn't wish to do? Did you never cozen your pet slave? Did you never kiss his feet? Yet if someone should compel you to kiss the feet of Caesar, you would regard that as insolence and most extravagant tyranny. What else, then, is slavery? (4.1.15–18)

This type of love enslaves a person's reason and better judgement to her passionate desire for her loved one; it results in a state of emotional bondage. The Stoic values her personal dignity and self-respect too much to let her affection take her volition hostage in this way. This is exactly why she takes deliberate steps to prevent her love of others from turning into an irrational *pathos* that overpowers her reason and throws her into a psychic slavery.

E. Only the sage truly loves

The difficulty of regulating one's love and affection so that they provide only positive, joyful feelings without making one emotionally dependent upon loved ones should by now be quite obvious. Epictetus' awareness of this difficulty is evident in his fascinating argument that in fact only the wise person (*phronimos*) really has the power to love (*philein*).

Whatever one is interested in one naturally loves. Now do people take an interest in things evil? Not at all. Well, and do they take an interest in things which in no respect concern them? No, not in these either. It remains, therefore, that they take an interest in good things only; and if they take an interest in them, they love them. Whoever, then, has knowledge of good things, would know how to love them too; but when one is unable to distinguish things good from things evil, and what is neither good nor evil from both the others, how could he take the next step and have the power to love? Accordingly, the power to love belongs to the wise person and to him alone. (2.22.1–3)[16]

The logic of this argument can be analyzed as follows.

(1) People are concerned with good, not evil things.

(2) If one is interested in a thing, then one is concerned with it.

(3) If one loves a thing, then one is interested in it.

(4) Hence if one loves a thing, then one is concerned with it in so far as it is good.

Epictetus then assumes that if one *succeeds* in loving a thing, then one must know in fact that it is a *good* thing. If one cannot discriminate between good, evil, and indifferent things, however, then one will not know *what* to love. And if one is ignorant of what to love, Epictetus infers that one will not know *how* to love either.

The wise person has knowledge of what is truly good (the virtues), what is truly evil (the vices), and what is indifferent (extra-prohairetic things). This leads the wise person to take an interest in what is noble, just, and honorable, and to work to promote them. Understanding of these things empowers the wise person with love.

On this conception, love is an active capacity to judge what is good and produce it.[17] Fromm echoes the spirit of Epictetus' Stoic perspective on love by conceiving of it essentially 'as a rational phenomenon, as the crowning achievement of maturity.'[18] Fromm describes the rational faith that energizes love. 'Rational faith is not primarily belief in something, but the quality of certainty and firmness which our convictions have. Faith is a character trait pervading the whole personality, rather than a specific belief.'[19] The certainty of disposition enjoyed by the wise person stems from a firm grasp of knowledge of good, evil, and what is neither, not mere belief in the apparent good. The Stoic wise person commits herself to loving others without expecting that that love be reciprocated. If the people she loves are not wise, after all, on Epictetus' account they lack the power to return her love.

On this account, then, the wise person loves others not primarily by striving to improve their material or economic conditions of living, but by transmitting to them her inner wealth, her wisdom.

Beyond the minimal necessities of water, food, clothing, and shelter, the Stoic wise person, the sage, offers humanitarian aid in the form of education. This is because although economic aid provides basic subsistence, it does not contribute to what Epictetus believes to be real happiness. Real happiness consists in internal goods, namely the virtues of character and mental freedom produced by wise judgements. Happiness can thus be seen as the fruit of Stoic education. This is precisely why Epictetus, as a teacher, is committed[20] to doing all he can to eliminate the mental and spiritual poverty that is the source of misery of non-Stoics. As Bonhöffer observes, this explains why the activity of the wise Cynic, the king of the *kosmos*, is so much more important than political activity pertaining to taxes and revenue (3.22.83; cf. 1.10.1).[21] Epictetus regards the Cynic as the greatest benefactor of the human race because of the moral improving and ennobling influence he has on his fellow-beings.[22] The wise Stoic sage thus loves by trying to teach Stoicism and encouraging others to gain her knowledge and emulate her – the possessor of perfect happiness and self-sufficiency.[23] In the final chapter we examine Epictetus' portrait of the sage.

Notes

1. I am using 'philanthropy' in the literal sense 'love of human beings.' One could as easily use 'benevolence' to refer to the 'love of thy neighbor.'

2. Oldfather's translation of 1.19.13–15: *katholou te toiautēn tēn phusin tou logikou zōiou kateskeuasen, hina mēdenos tōn idiōn agathōn dunētai tunchanein, an mē ti eis to koinon ōphelimon prospherētai. Houtōs ouketi akoinōnēton ginetai to panta hautou heneka poiein. Epei ti ekdechēi? hina tis apostei hautou kai tou idiou sumpherontos? kai pōs eti mia kai hē autē archē pasin estai hē pros hauta oikeiōsis?*

3. See D. L. 7.85–7.86.1 will discuss *oikeiōsis* at length in Chapter 4.

4. Bonhöffer writes '... Epictet es keineswegs dem Belieben des einzelnen anheimstellt, ob er in die Ehe treten will oder nicht,

sondern da er die Ehe als die einzige legitime Art und Weise
der Fortpflanzung des menschlichen Geschlechts und letztere,
seinem Optimismus gemäss, selbstverständlich als sittliche
Aufgabe betrachtet, so muss er auch in der Ehe eine Pflicht
des Menschen erblicken, von der nur besondere Umstände
dispensieren können' (Bonhöffer, 1894: 86); my translation:
'... Epictetus by no means leaves it to the preference of the
individual whether he wants to enter into marriage or not. But
since he considers marriage as the only legitimate type and
mode of the propagation of the human race and the latter
is, according to his optimism, obviously a moral task, so must
he also perceive in marriage a person's duty, from which only
special circumstances could exempt.'

5. My translation of: 'Es ist klar, dass die Pflicht selbstloser liebe
    mit dem Eudämonismus nur dann zusammen bestehen kann,
    wenn die Liebe als eine wesentliche Qualität des Geistigen
    selbst erkannt wird, so dass die Uebung der Liebe nur als ein
    Stück der geistigen Selbsterhaltung erscheint. Dies spricht
    nun eben Epictet so deutlich als möglich aus, indem er den
    Eudämonismus vom Egoismus (*philanton*) scharf unterscheidet,
    die altruistischen Pflichten unter die im höheren Sinn
    egoistischen subsumiert und den Satz aufstellt: Gott hat die
    Natur des Verrnunftwesens so eingerichtet, dass es keines
    der ihn eigentümlichen Güter erlangen kann, wenn es nicht
    zugleich gemeinnützig ist (I, 19, 13).' (Bonhöffer, 1894: 158)

6. My translation of: 'Der Trieb zu thatkräftiger hingebender
    Arbeit an der Beseitigung des menschlichen Elends wird
    notwendig geschwächt durch die übertriebene Verachtung
    aller irdischen Glücksgüter' (Bonhöffer, 1894: 159).

7. My translation of: '... den ökonomischen und kulturellen Aufgaben
    des Gemeinwesensein wirkliches Interesse entgegenzubringen.
    Bei dem allem muss aber zugegeben werden, dass sie, wenn
    auch vielleicht mit einer gewissen Inkonsequenz, den Wert
    der Vaterlandsliebe und die Pflicht des gemeinnützigen

Wirkens eifrig verteidigt und es den Ihrigen für den Fall, dass sie ein öffentliches Amt bekleideten, zur Pflicht gemacht haben, mit aller Treue und Gewissenhaftigkeit für die allgemeine Wohlfahrt zu sorgen.' (Bonhöffer, 1894: 94)

8. My translation of: 'Wer dem Vaterland nicht durch Bekleidung von Aemtern oder durch finanzielle Opfer dienen kann, mag es dadurch thun, dass er durch sein Wort und Beispiel auf seine Mitbürger bessernd einwirkt: dadurch nützt er ihm mehr als wenn er Säulenhallen und Bäder erstellt' (Bonhöffer, 1894: 95).

9. As a Stoic, Epictetus rejects the Epicurean claim that pleasure is the object of a living being's primary impulse.

10. This was pointed out to me in discussion with Timothy Mahoney.

11. Annas (1990: 83).

12. Michael Frede makes this same point by observing that the Stoics reject the Aristotelian view of the *pathē* because 'they also think it is grossly misleading to think of the affections of the soul as *pathē* in the sense of passive affections. They rather are *pathē* in the sense of illnesses, diseases. Indeed, they are the diseases of the mind which we have to cure' (Frede, 1986: 93).

13. My translation of 'Der Eros ist also hier als eine den inneren Frieden und das wahre Glück störende Gemütsbewegung aufgefasst' (Bonhöffer, 1894: 66).

14. Frede's account of the position of the Stoics in general on this point accurately applies to Epictetus: '... they claim that the affections have their origin in a judgment of reason, or even that they themselves are judgments of reason, namely misjudgments to the effect that something is good or bad when, in fact, it is neither, but completely indifferent' (Frede, 1986: 100).

15. My translation of: 'Der Stoiker der mitseufzt, braucht also dabei seine richtige Anschauung nicht zu verleugnen, vielmehr wird er alles thun, um den Leidenden zu beruhigen und zur Standhaftigkeit zu ermuntern. Wo dies nicht möglich ist,

wird er seine Menschenliebe dadurch zeigen, dass er sich wenigstens Scheinbar auf den Standpunkt des Leidenden stellt. Zudem wird der Stoiker ja mit dem Leidenden immerhin ein gewisses Bedauern empfinden, weniger wegen seines äusseren Leidens als wegen seiner inneren Schwäche und Verblendung. Dieses vernünftige Bedauern, das also sozusagen nur intellektueller, nicht gemütlicher Natur ist, äussert Epictet nicht selten.' (Bonhöffer 1894: 102–3)

16. Cf. Paracelsus 'He who knows nothing, loves nothing. He who can do nothing understands nothing. He who understands nothing is worthless. But he who understands also loves, notices, sees. ... The more knowledge is inherent in a thing, the greater the love.'

17. The parallels between the accounts of love articulated by Epictetus and Erich Fromm are striking: 'To love somebody is not just a strong feeling – it is a decision, it is a judgment, it is a promise. ... Love should be essentially an act of will, of decision to commit my life completely to that of one other person' (Fromm, 1974: 47).

18. Fromm (1974: 76).

19. Fromm (1974: 102).

20. Fromm's view resonates with aspects of Epictetus' view: 'To love means to commit oneself without guarantee, to give oneself completely in the hope that our love will produce love in the loved person. Love is an act of faith, and whoever is of little faith is also of little love' (Fromm, 1974: 107).

21. Bonhöffer (1894: 95).

22. Bonhöffer (1894: 105).

23. See Stephens (1996b).

Chapter 4

Happiness as freedom

In the previous chapters we have examined: (a) Epictetus' concept of the *prohairesis* (volition) as the true, inner self; (b) how the *dogmata* (judgements) issued by the *prohairesis* determine its moral condition and one's consequent happiness or misery; (c) what the proper attitude toward and treatment of external objects must be to preserve the Stoic's healthy, serene state of mind; (d) what behavior toward other people is appropriate for the Stoic; and (e) how the Stoic can freely love others without falling prey to emotional servitude.

Several questions remain. What exactly is the Stoic sage? In section A I will propose that for Epictetus the sage represents a prescriptive ideal that epitomizes the *telos* (final end) as the one who makes perfect rational use of her *prohairesis*. This discussion will generate the following question. Given that for the Stoics the *telos*, happiness or the good, is a life according to nature (where 'nature' is to be taken teleologically), why is this life *kata phusin* necessarily the life of *logos* (reason), that is, the ongoing, rigorous exercise of one's *prohairesis*? For example, why is the preservation of our pre-rational animal nature or the pursuit of fame and power not instead an essential part of the good life? Addressing these questions will occupy the first stage of the argument (section B).

In outline, the second stage of the argument will be this. Given that the life of reason and moral judgement is established, by the first stage of the argument, as the life according to nature, why is the content of rational judgement and *prohairesis* determined by virtue and the *kathēkonta* (proper functions)? In other words, why are respect, honor, fidelity, benevolence, etc., as required by our roles and obligations, constitutive of the life according to reason (i.e. the correct use of the *prohairesis*) rather than a non-moral life of egoism or self-preservation narrowly understood? I will grapple with these issues in section C. In the course of working out the Stoic 'solutions' to these problems, I will extrapolate beyond the *Diatribae* since, although some of Epictetus' remarks are suggestive of Stoic arguments based on the doctrine of *oikeiōsis*, he does not offer them explicitly. In the course of this exposition the respects in which the Stoic strategies conflict with the positions of Aristotle and Epicurus will emerge.

The relationship between happiness (*eudaimonia*) and unperturbedness (*ataraxia*) and a discussion of the anti-Stoic will occupy section D. I will conclude with an overall assessment of the strengths and weaknesses of what I take to be the most salient features of Epictetus' ethical thought. I begin by presenting my interpretation of Epictetus' portrait of the sage in order to view his ethical system in the proper light.

A. The sage as prescriptive ideal

Epictetus announces to his students that his goal as a teacher of Stoicism is 'to make of you a perfect work, secure against restraint, compulsion, and hindrance, free, prosperous, happy, looking to god in everything both small and great' (2.19.29). His audaciously ambitious goal is to transform them into perfectly invulnerable paragons of human excellence free from hindrance, worry, and grief, impervious to coercion, and ready to accede to god's will in everything. Such a person's happiness would be immune to reversal by any worldly situation.

> Show me someone who though sick is happy, though in danger is happy, though dying is happy, though condemned to exile is happy, though in disrepute is happy. Show him! By the gods, I would fain see a Stoic! But you cannot show me someone completely so fashioned; then show me at least one who is becoming so fashioned, one who has begun to tend in that direction; do me this favour; do not begrudge an old man the

sight of that spectacle which to this very day I have never seen. (2.19.24–5)

An individual capable of being happy in the conditions of life that cause most to be hopelessly miserable would seem to be rare beyond belief. Epictetus wants to see someone so fervently committed to maintaining the intensity of mental discipline needed to be a Stoic that he is at least making discernible progress toward that goal.[1]
Epictetus continues:

> Let one of you show me the soul of a person who wishes to be of one mind with god, and never again to blame either god or human, to fail in nothing that he would achieve, to fall into nothing that he would avoid, to be free from anger, envy and jealousy – but why use circumlocutions? – one who has set his heart upon changing from a human being into a god. And although he is still in this paltry body of death, does nonetheless have his purpose set upon fellowship with Zeus. (2.19.26–7)

The kind of individual described here has resolved to become a being lacking in nothing, perfect, completely sufficient unto himself, a god. To want to be a Stoic is to be dissatisfied with one's own human weaknesses and to want to be superhuman. To strive to be a Stoic is to labor at self-deification.[2] Yet a desire to be superhuman could easily be construed as an unsubtle sign of misanthropy.[3] Epictetus, however, sees dissatisfaction with others' human failings and with the world's arrangement as the cause of anger and fault-finding. Harmonious satisfaction with the world as it is, on the other hand, is what Epictetus sees as the means of liberation from malcontentment and petty blaming. The true Stoic has an invincible character and tireless spirit, not a body immune to degeneration and death.

> Of such character will I show myself to you – faithful, reverent, noble, unperturbed. You do not mean, therefore, immortal, or ageless, or exempt from disease? No, but one who dies like a god, who bears disease like a god. This is what I have; this is what

I can do; but all else I neither have nor can do. I will show you the sinews of a philosopher. What do you mean sinews? A desire that fails not of achievement, an aversion proof against encountering what it would avoid, an appropriate choice, a thoughtful purpose, a well-considered assent. This is what you shall see. (2.8.27–9)

To bear all that befalls him in his mortal life with equanimity and nobility, displaying his divine serenity even in sickness unto death – this, Epictetus insists, and this alone is within his power. These virtues of character and the power to make the correct decisions are all he really has as his own.

A *spoudaios* is a person who is deeply serious about being a perfect Stoic, i.e. the 'sage.' Although Epictetus' hope is to behold one such *spoudaios*, he says he would settle for seeing someone who is progressing toward that stage (2.19.25). He does not erect this model of perfection as a ridiculously unrealistic, unrealizable ideal. Rather, he sets it up as a target which the perfectionist can concentrate on aiming at. 'What then? Is it possible to be free from fault altogether? No, that cannot be achieved, but it is possible ever to be intent upon avoiding faults. For we must be satisfied, if we succeed in escaping at least a few faults by never relaxing our attention' (4.12.19). It is not possible *for us*[4] to be faultless, but we can *try* to be faultless by remaining vigilant in everything we do. We must be satisfied as long as we constantly strive for psychic perfection. Active, earnest desire for mental perfection and diligent attention to all our tasks make progress toward the ideal achievable.

Where, then, is progress? If one of you, withdrawing from external things, has turned his attention to the question of his own volition, cultivating and perfecting it so as to make it finally harmonious with nature, elevated, free, unhindered, untrammelled, faithful, and honourable; and if he has learned that he who craves or shuns the things that are not up to him can be neither faithful (*pistos*) nor free, but must himself of necessity be changed and tossed to and fro with them, and must end by subordinating himself to others, those, namely, who are able to procure or prevent these things that he craves or shuns; and if, finally, when he rises in the morning he proceeds to keep and observe all this that he has learned; if he bathes as one faithful, eats as one self-respecting (*aidēmon*), similarly, whatever the subject matter may be with which he has to deal, putting into practice his guiding principles, as the runner does when he applies the principles of running, and the voice-trainer when he applies the principles of voice-training, this is the one who in all truth is making progress, and the one who has not travelled at random is this one. (1.4.18–21)

The one making progress (the *prokoptōn*[5]) actually actively applies the principles of Stoicism in practice; she does not merely mouth them as theoretic truths. Her progress is manifested not in what she has learned in class, but in how she lives in the world.

Signs of one who is making progress are: He censures no one, praises no one, blames no one, finds fault with no one, says nothing about himself as though he were somebody or knew something. When he is hampered or prevented, he blames himself. And if anyone compliments him, he smiles to himself at the person complimenting; while if anyone censures him, he makes no defense. He goes about like an invalid, being careful not to disturb, before it has grown firm, any part which is getting well. He has put away from himself his every desire, and has transferred his aversion to those things only, of what is up to him, which are contrary to nature. He exercises no pronounced choice in regard to anything. If he gives the appearance of being foolish or ignorant he does not care. In a word, he keeps guard against himself as though he were his own enemy lying in wait. (*Ench.* 48.2–3)

The *prokoptōn* is in a fragile state since, although she is progressing toward the stage of perfection epitomized by the sage, she is not there yet. Thus she must be especially on guard so as not to slip up and fall into error – she must never relax her attention (4.12.19). Her moral steadfastness is firming up; yet it is not fully fixed. This is why she goes about with great caution like an 'invalid.'

But is her invalidity and foolishness just an appearance? Or is it indicative of the philosophy of a slave with no worldly, material power? Epictetus contends that the same thing, the *prohairesis*, is under the control of everyone, slave and emperor alike. In the material, extra-prohairetic world, real and severe inequalities of power obviously exist. The Stoic holds that the master, e.g. the emperor, does not really have more power than the slave, but is just able to indulge his slavish desires (for externals) and vain aspirations better. This is a slave's ethic. The point of moral agency is to be in control (the slave's *ressentiment*); but the slave and the emperor, his master, have the same capacity for control.[6]

The Stoic slave could respond to this penetrating criticism as follows. I cannot win out in the extra-prohairetic, material world since my master owns my body and can treat it, beat it, or starve it as he will. Thus I will not compete against him materially by combating him with my body. Instead I will ensure myself victory in my choices, my purposes, and my mental world. Here he has no power over me. Here I am free to win by willing. There (in the material world) he can 'win' by killing me, but he cannot defeat my spirit if I refuse to let him.

Epictetus is fully aware of the difficulty involved in perfecting one's character by totally embracing and living the ethical tenets of Stoicism. The resolve and self-discipline required are extraordinary.[7] Yet he is convinced that these Stoic judgements are the salvation of the individual, the family, the state, and the peoples of the world. Thus

> ... this control over the volition is my true business, and in it neither shall a tyrant hinder me against my will, nor the multitude the single individual, nor the stronger man the weaker; for this has been given by god to each as something that cannot be hindered. These are the judgements that produce love in the household, concord in the state, peace among the nations, make one thankful toward god, confident at all times, on the ground that he is dealing with things not his own, with worthless things. We, however, although we are capable of

writing and reading these things, and praising them when read, are *nowhere near* capable of being persuaded of them. (4.5.34–6; my emphasis)

Stoic judgements are the best, yet Epictetus regrets that we somehow cannot bring ourselves to take them to heart and adopt them. He sees this inability as a shortcoming in us, however, not in the judgements themselves.[8]

Epictetus is a keen enough observer of human beings to recognize that the vast majority of people have neither the mettle nor the desire to be Stoics.

Observe yourselves thus in your actions and you will find out to what sect of the philosophers you belong. You will find that most of you are Epicureans, some few Peripatetics, but these without any backbone (*eklelumenous*); for wherein do you in fact show that you consider virtue equal to all things else, or even superior? But as for a Stoic, show me one if you can! Where, or how? Nay, but you can show me thousands who recite the petty arguments of the Stoics. (2.19.20–2)

Many can recite Stoic judgements, but does anyone genuinely live by them?

Epictetus' pride in Stoicism shows in the following passage where he addresses the person who fears the emperor more than he values integrity and dignity:

... you regard yourself as but a single thread of all that go to make up the garment. What follows, then? This, that *you* ought to take thought how you may resemble all other people, precisely as even the single thread wants to have no point of superiority in comparison with the other threads. But *I* want to be the red, that small and brilliant portion that causes the rest to appear comely and beautiful. Why, then, do you say to me, 'Be like the majority[9] of people?' And if I do that, how shall I any longer be the red? (Oldfather's emphasis of 1.2.17–18; cf. 1.2.22)

This quotation is essential for establishing that Epictetus believes Stoicism is for the *few*, not the many. The person who values her moral integrity and dignity above all else differentiates herself from the many Epicureans, who judge pleasure (the absence of pain) to be the good, and Peripatetics, who judge virtue to be a necessary but not a sufficient condition of the good life. The Stoic, in judging virtue to be sufficient for the good life, is conspicuous. She stands out from non-Stoics like the bright red stripe on the hem of the *toga praetexta*. It is interesting in this passage that Epictetus thinks that the few red threads – perhaps precisely *because* they are few – contrast with the other threads and thereby beautify the whole garment. This would seem to cohere with his remarks that the universe is well organized by Zeus in containing summer *and* winter, abundance *and* dearth, virtue *and* vice, for the harmony of the whole (1.12.16). The beauty of the toga lies in the harmonious contrast between the red stripe and the non-red threads, just as the beauty of humanity lies in the philosophical opposition between Stoics and non-Stoics, be they Epicureans, Peripatetics, skeptics, hedonists, or of some other camp.

Epictetus thinks that if one could only subscribe heart and soul to the Stoic doctrine that all are begotten of god and that the god is the father of humans and gods alike, 'I think he will entertain no ignoble or mean thought about himself' (1.3.1). His dualistic ontology is reminiscent of Aristotle when he observes that though we have reason (*logos*) and intelligence (*gnōmē*) in common with the gods, we also have bodies in common with animals (*zōa*). Some of us, he continues, incline to the latter unblessed and mortal element, while only a few of us incline to that which is blessed and divine (1.3.3).

> Since, then, it is inevitable that each person, whoever he be, should deal with each thing according to the opinion that he forms about it, these few, who think that by their birth they are called to fidelity, to self-respect, and to unerring judgement in the use of impressions (*phantasiōn*), cherish no mean or ignoble thoughts about themselves, whereas the multitude do quite the opposite. (1.3.4)

His judgement, which probably derives from empirical observations, is that the multitude judge themselves wretched because they judge their physical condition to be wretched. They are not cheered by the divinity of their rational powers. In contrast, the self-respect of the few who are predisposed to be Stoics precludes them from compromising their moral excellence. But only a rare few, as it turns out, have the prowess to stand out from the crowd like this (cf. 1.2.30–2 and 3.1.22–3).

Epictetus, we can see, erects the Stoic sage as a prescriptive ideal that it is rational for a few to emulate as much as is humanly possible. The tremendous rigors of self-discipline are such that only a few have the disposition and resolve to make progress toward this ethical ideal; yet *progress is possible.* Moreover, there are several who came so close that they might even have reached the final stage of moral perfection. Epictetus cites Socrates,[10] the founder of the Stoa Zeno, and Cleanthes as exemplars (3.23.32), and he holds up Socrates and Zeno as model Stoics (*Ench.* 33.12). He also points to Diogenes the Cynic as an ethical model (1.24.6–10; *Ench.* 15; cf. *Discourses* 3.22). Epictetus cites Diogenes as an example of someone who was truly free (3.24.67; 4.1.114; 4.1.152). He often refers to the equanimity of Socrates and Diogenes (2.13.24; 2.16.35–6; cf. 4.9.6), and how they were models of Stoic loving (3.24.60–5) and Stoic living (3.26.23; 4.1.159ff.). Elsewhere he reminds us not to put stock in the opinions of just anyone, but that only the judgements of a Socrates or a Diogenes should matter to us (4.7.29; *Ench.* 5). 'And even if you are not yet a Socrates, still you ought to live as one who wishes to be a Socrates' (*Ench.* 51.3). Socrates, whom Epictetus reveres as his moral hero, is someone we ought to emulate as best we can (2.6.26; 3.7.34). For Epictetus, Socrates is the best paragon of the Stoic wise man (3.5.14–19; 4.5.1–4).

We cannot be Socrates, but we can try to be, so to speak, as Stoic as he was.

Only consider at what price you sell your self (*prohairesis*). If you must sell it, man (*anthrōpos*), at least do not sell it cheap. But the great and pre-eminent deed, perhaps, befits others, Socrates and those of his kind. – Why then, if we are endowed by nature for such greatness, do not all or many become like him? What, do all horses become swift, all dogs keen to follow the scent? What then? Because I have no natural gifts, shall I on that account give up my discipline? Far be it from me! Epictetus will not be better than Socrates; but only if I am not worse, that suffices me. For I shall not be a Milo, either, and yet I do not neglect my body; nor a Croesus, and yet I do not neglect my property; nor, in a word, is there any other field in which we give up the appropriate discipline merely from despair of attaining the highest (1.2.33–7).[11]

All human beings have been endowed by nature with the capacity to develop and perfect their virtues of character, yet only a few will excel. One must do one's best to train, improve, and strengthen all of one's human excellences. To the extent we succeed in modeling our art of living after the prescriptive ideal of the sage, to that extent we achieve *eudaimonia* as Epictetus understands it. Though we may well never reach perfection, for a few to make some progress toward it is possible. Not to want to make the effort is, as we will see in sections C and D below, not to want to be *eudaimōn*. For Epictetus this laziness is symptomatic of an unhealthy, flabby, obtuse self.

But the sage, it must be stressed, is infallible and unbeatable only within the sphere that matters to her, the prohairetic sphere. All externals she willingly cedes to those who scramble for them.

> The sage (*ho spoudaios*) is invincible; naturally, for he enters no contest where he is not superior. 'If you want my property in the country,' says he, 'take it; take my servants, take my office, take my paltry body. But you will not make my desire fail to get what I will, nor my aversion fall into what I would avoid.' This is the only contest into which he enters, one, namely, that is concerned with volitional things; how, then, can he help but be invincible? (3.6.5–7)

The sage does not contend for objects. The sage strives relentlessly for freedom from her desires for externals. Unencumbered by psychological investment in contingent, extra-prohairetic affairs, the sage, as a moral agent, is invincible.

B. Life according to nature as the life of reason

Epictetus follows orthodox Stoic doctrine in defining the final end, the *summum bonum* for human beings, as living *kata phusin* (in accordance with nature) (3.24.101–2) or *kata phusin echein* (1.12.19; 1.20.2; 3.10.10; 4.5.5). 'But what is it I want? To learn nature and to follow her' (*Ench.* 49). He also describes it as being in harmony with nature (*symphōnōs tēi phusei*) (1.4.15, 18, and 29). 'For if you are acting in harmony, show me that, and I will tell you that you are making progress' (1.4.15). He variously urges us *kata phusin echein tēn dianoian* (3.9.17), to keep *to hēgemonikon kata phusin* (1.15.4; 3.6.3; 3.9.11; 3.10.11; 4.4.43; and cf. 3.5.3), to keep our *prohairesis kata phusin* (3.4.9; *Ench.* 13 and 30), and to use *phantasiai kata phusin* (3.26.15; 4.4.14). Thus he insists: 'I will convince you that whatever is done in accordance with nature is rightly done' (1.11.6).

Thus nature represents the norm for human thought and conduct. What notion of nature can justify this role as the ultimate moral principle? Epictetus, like all Stoics, Plato, and Aristotle as well, has a teleological and normative conception of nature. That is why he says 'everything's evil is what is contrary to its own nature (*to para tēn ekeinou phusin*)' (4.1.125; cf. 4.1.121–2). Consequently, Epictetus lays down the following '... law of life – that we must do what nature demands. For if we wish in every matter and circumstance to observe what is in accordance with nature, it is manifest that in everything we should make it our aim neither to avoid that which nature demands, nor to accept that which is in conflict with nature' (1.26.1–2; cf. 3.13.20). This, however, raises questions. What does 'accordance with nature' amount to? What does nature demand?

Although this phrase '*kata phusin*' may strike the modern thinker as hopelessly vague and potentially vacuous, it is central to understanding Stoic ethics, and its meaning is in fact both rich and definite. In Epictetus we can distinguish five different meanings of the word '*phusis*'[12]: (1) kind, essence, sort (e.g. the 'nature' of poverty, exile, or death); (2) the universe seen as an ordered whole (*kosmos*) determined by a principle of structure (*logos*) and law (*nomos*); Nature (capitalized) in this sense

Epictetus identifies with god (Zeus); (3) particular nature, the law of nature in the individual organism as it were localized and particularized, the constitution of an organism (e.g. the 'nature' of a dog, snake, or tree); (4) human nature, which is properly only a special kind of particular nature, in so far as it is common to all members of *Homo sapiens sapiens*; (5) one's unique set of traits as an individual (e.g. Epictetus' 'nature' as a lame ex-slave and gifted teacher).

The Stoic, for example, knows what sort of thing death is in sense (1); she knows what it is and thus that it is not to be feared as an evil. The Stoic conforms her will to Nature in sense (2) by accepting and embracing everything that happens in the universe (as discussed in Chapter 2). All animals and plants by nature in sense (3) function as organisms that metabolize water and nourishment and expel waste. Human beings by nature in sense (4) possess *logos* and live in communities. By nature in sense (5), one person is endowed with a wrestler's physique, another has a talent for music, and yet another skill for oratory.

At this point we must look beyond Arrian's *Diatribae* in order to understand properly Epictetus' conception of nature in the broader context of the Stoic tradition, where its meaning is fleshed out by the concept of *oikeiōsis*. The Stoics employed their doctrine of *oikeiōsis* to support their argument that virtue is the sole necessary and sufficient condition of *eudaimonia*, the final end. Hence we must now sketch an account of this doctrine.

First of all, what does the term *oikeiōsis* mean? It is indirectly derived from the adjective *oikeios*, 'akin, one's own,' by way of the verb *oikeiousthai* 'to make something one's own, to appropriate it.' Hence a lexicon's list of meanings of *oikeiōsis* includes 'appropriation,' but also 'affinity,' 'attraction,' 'affection,' 'propensity,' and 'becoming familiar with.'[13] In an important study of this concept Pembroke claims that in the Stoa: '*oikeiōsis* is never used in the active sense of appropriation. What it denotes is a relationship, but this is not bilateral, and it is the subjective factor, the consciousness of such a relationship – which does not have to be reciprocated – on which most emphasis is placed.'[14] Pembroke also rejects 'endearment' as a translation because it inappropriately sentimentalizes the idea, and she instead favors 'well-disposed' for *oikeiousthai*.[15] Striker holds that *oikeiōsis* '... can perhaps be rendered as "recognition and appreciation of something as belonging to one"; the corresponding verb, which is actually more prominent in the earlier sources, *oikeiousthai pros ti*, as "coming to be (or being made to be) well-disposed toward something"'.[16] Long and Sedley instead opt for 'appropriation':

> This connotes ownership, what belongs to something, but in Stoic usage that notion is also conceived as an affective disposition relative to the thing which is owned or belongs. Hence the English associations of 'appropriation' with forcible possession are to be discounted in our translations.[17]

Annas follows Jonathan Barnes' suggestion of 'familiarization' to render this difficult word: 'The verb *oikeioō* introduces a three-term relation: A familiarizes B with C.'[18] In view of the scholarly debate over how best to capture in English the subtle meanings of this term, I will simply transliterate it.

The argument in which *oikeiōsis* is used to establish the *telos* for human beings is not fully stated in any single source. Striker reconstructs it largely from Seneca's *Epistulae ad Lucilium*, while Engberg-Pedersen[19] uses Cicero, *De Finibus* Book III. The argument is basically this:

1. The *prōton oikeion*, the first thing recognized as belonging to one, is one's own self or constitution (*sustasis*). This holds for all creatures, including human beings. *Sustasis* would include *phusis* in both sense 3 (4 for humans) and sense 5 here.
2. The first impulse for every creature will thus be for preservation, care, and nurture of this self. Love of self becomes the one basic evaluative fact.[20]
3. Each creature matures and develops, but for most the recognition of itself (*sustasis*) does not change significantly because it remains largely the same. However, once a human being reaches the age of *logos*, in its case, concern for itself will be concern for a rational animal (in sense 4).

Engberg-Pedersen describes the mechanism of *oikeiōsis* as follows:

> A man loves himself. But this means that he loves whatever he takes himself to be. Now a grown up man is (also) rational and he cannot but see that he is. So he will come to love 'his' reason. And from this it follows that he will come to adopt any insights reached by reason as his own: he will necessarily believe them as being valid for himself too.[21]

But to be '*also*' rational does not establish that one is *only* rational. Hence it does not follow that the adult human will love *only* her reason.

On Frede's account of this Stoic position, however, the newly developed faculty of rationality squeezes out the non-rational, animalistic element and becomes the sole object of concern. Platonists and Peripatetics, he writes,

> ... think that since nature from birth has endowed us with certain natural inclinations and disinclinations the objects of these natural impulses must be goods and evils. Hence their behaviour comes to be motivated, not by instinctive impulses, but by affections of the soul, namely their assent to impulsive impressions in which the objects of the natural inclinations with which we are born are represented as good or bad. But little do they realise that not everything which is conducive to the survival of something, even be it oneself, for that mere reason is good. Nor do they appreciate the fact that the natural instinctive impulses of animals are meant to help them to maintain their existence as animals. But since we no longer are animals, but are rational beings now, it seems even more absurd to think of the things which were of importance for our survival as animals as goods or as evils. What we should now be concerned with is what is conducive or detrimental to our rationality, to our survival as rational beings. As we become rational we are supposed to realise that there is a natural order of things of which we are just a part, that we from birth have been constructed in such a way as to help maintain this natural order and to maintain it by

means of reason, once we have become rational, and that it is hence the most rational thing for us to do to try as well as we can to maintain this order, since, given that everything is fated, we cannot act against its design anyway.[22]

That Frede's account accurately describes Epictetus' teleology is evident from the following dense passage.

> The god had need of the (non-rational) animals in that they make use of impressions (*phantasiai*), and of us in that we understand the use of impressions. And so for them it is enough to eat and drink and rest and procreate, and whatever else of the things within their own province the animals severally do; while for us, to whom he has made the additional gift of the faculty of understanding, these things are no longer enough, but unless we act appropriately, and methodically, and in conformity each with his own nature and constitution, we shall no longer achieve our own ends. For of beings whose constitutions are different, the works and the ends (*ta erga kai ta telē*) are likewise different. So for the being whose constitution is adapted to use only, mere use is enough, but where a being has also the faculty of understanding the use, unless the way of living (i.e. understanding the use) be added, he will never attain his end. What then? Each of the animals he constitutes, one to be eaten, another to serve in farming, another to produce cheese, and yet another for some other similar use; to perform these functions what need have they to understand impressions and to be able to differentiate between them? But the god has brought the human being into the world to be a spectator of himself and of his works, and not merely a spectator, but also an interpreter. Wherefore, it is shameful for the human being to begin and end just where the non-rational animals do; he should rather begin where they do, but end where nature has ended in dealing with us. Now she did not end until she reached contemplation and understanding and a manner of life harmonious with nature. Therefore, see to it that you don't die without ever having been spectators of these things. (1.6.13–22)

Epictetus believes that we have the power to scrutinize *phantasiai* and self-consciously use them for certain ends. Our ability to direct our use of these impressions toward our self-determined ends is something we ought not to ignore. We have intelligence and understanding for a reason. Nature intends us to exercise our mental capacities with propriety, not to abuse them. Having developed from pre-rational children, i.e. mere spectators of the world, into mature, rational adults, i.e. fully self-conscious interpreters of the world, we learn how world-transforming our adult human capacities really are.

Before the dawn of reason (at age 14) *oikeiōsis* amounted to maintaining an organism that wants food, drink, and comfort. Preservation of this organism involved calculation, but no concern for propriety at all. Upon the dawn of reason, however, our *sustasis* transforms. The pre-rational self had only animalistic desires. But now the self is not primarily an organism wanting food, drink, and comfort *simpliciter*, but rather an interpreting self, a thinking, deciding, and intending self, i.e. a *prohairesis*. We are thus in a position to interpret our special human capacities as those which we, in so far as we are to function as persons, instead of simply as mammals, are to use. The life according to nature for normal adult human beings is the life of reason because reason is the special power with which we are equipped. If we fail to actualize our rational faculties by exercising our *prohairesis* so as to make the proper *rational* use of our impressions, then we fail to function as persons. We nullify that part of ourselves that differentiates us from non-self-conscious beings. It would be to live the life of an owl or an eel, not a human being. Mere use of impressions befits owls and eels. But appropriate, methodical use of my impressions, in conformity with my nature (a) as a mammal (sense 3 taken broadly), (b) as a human being (sense 4), and (c) as Bill Stephens (sense 5), allows me to achieve my ends (a) as an animal that needs food, drink, and comfort, (b) as an adult that needs love, companionship, and social solidarity within human society, and (c) as a self-determining, unique person.

At this point we must return to the foregoing argument in order to reflect on an important point. I objected to the inference that once human beings reach the age of reason, concern for self then becomes concern *exclusively* for the rationality of the self. Striker reasons

... if man's concern for rationality is a form of concern for himself, why should he come to completely neglect his animal nature? After all, physical well-being should still be a natural concern for him, since he still has both body and soul, so why should he care for the one, and not at all for the other? Why, indeed, should a new concern that arises out of man's psychological development supplant rather than supplement earlier ones?[23] Why, one quite reasonably asks, should the demands of the body, including food, drink, sex, clothing, and shelter, suddenly cease to count as true goods to the Stoic once she reaches the age of reason, while she has been pursuing them all out of love of self since birth? Striker's reply to this objection to the Stoic theory seems fairly plausible: '... once we have come to realize that what makes our natural, instinctive behaviour good or right is its accord with nature, we will come to care more about accordance with nature than about the results of our various activities'.[24] For Epictetus food is not something one need worry about in comparison with one's goodness.

Does a good man (*anēr*) fear that food will fail him? It does not fail the blind, it does not fail the lame; will it fail a good man? A good soldier does not lack someone to pay him, or a workman, or a cobbler; shall a good person? Does the god so neglect his own creatures, his servants, his witnesses, whom alone he uses as examples to the uninstructed, to prove that he both is, and governs the universe well, and does not neglect the affairs of human beings, and that no evil befalls a good man (*anēr*) either in life or in death? – Yes, but what if he does not provide food? – Why, what else but that as a good general he has sounded the recall? I obey, I follow, lauding my commander, and singing hymns of praise about his deeds. (3.26.27–9)

Of course one who does not share Epictetus' trust in divine providence would naturally be disinclined to acquiesce to starving to
death.

In this passage Epictetus rather atypically uses the locution
'good man' (*agathos anēr*) instead of 'good human being' (*agathos
anthrōpos*). This does not indicate that the virtue of a good man
excludes that of a good woman. 'According to the Stoic teachings,
the moral virtues are the same for everyone without discrimination
of sex, race, or social condition.'[25]

Now we return to the privileged importance of rationality.
Rationality is our true good because it is what distinguishes us from
the other animals. But 'right reason' (*orthos logos*), in separating
us from non-rational beings, makes us akin to god. The god is
beneficial; but the good also is

> ... beneficial. It would seem, therefore, that the true nature
> (*ousia*) of the good will be found to be where we find that of
> the god to be. What, then, is the true nature of god? Flesh? Far
> from it! Land? Far from it! Fame? Far from it! It is intelligence,
> knowledge, right reason. Here, therefore, and only here shall
> you seek the true nature of the good. Surely you do not seek it
> at all in a plant, do you? No. Nor in a non-rational creature? No.
> If, then, you seek it in that which is rational, why do you keep on
> seeking it somewhere else than in that which differentiates the
> rational from the non-rational? (2.8.1–3; cf. also 3.1.25–6 and
> 4.11.33)

On Epictetus' conception of nature in following one's particular
nature as a human being (in sense 4 above), one is following
reason, since that is the distinctive endowment we have from
Nature (in sense 2). Thus in living in accordance with our
human nature we are also living in accordance with universal
nature, that is, *orthos logos*.[26] But on the theological view,[27] all of
Nature is providentially organized by the supreme being, 'God.' So
when Epictetus defines the final end (*telos*)[28] both as following the
gods (1.12.5 and 1.20.15) and as keeping *ton logon orthon* (4.8.12),
we can see that he is conflating the secular and the theological

views. This is to say either that for Epictetus the one amounts to the other, or else he does not bother to separate secular teleology from theological personification of divine providence.

Epictetus repeats the idea that in life we must act as if we were dutiful soldiers on campaign by obeying every assignment of our commander, the god (3.24.31–3): '... the life of each is a kind of campaign, and a long and complicated one at that. You have to maintain the character of a soldier, and do each separate act at the bidding of the general, if possible divining what he wishes' (3.24.34–5). Similarly he uses a theatrical metaphor:

> Remember that you are an actor in a play, the character of which is determined by the playwright: if he wishes the play to be short, it is short; if long, it is long; if he wants you to play the part of a beggar, remember to act even this role adroitly; and so if your role be that of a cripple, an official, or a layman. For this is your business, to play admirably the role assigned to you; but the selection of that role is another's. (*Ench.* 17)

In passages such as these, Epictetus' theological teleology stands out more prominently than ever. The divine plan of the universe pervades each and every thing, plant, animal, and person (cf. 1.14.1–9). Nature (sense 2) is decidedly purposive, and it (the universe = Zeus) dictates our proper functions. Death is not an end, but by its nature (sense 1) it is merely a change into

> ... something different from that of which the universe now has need. And this is but reasonable, for you came into being not when *you* wanted, but when the universe had need of you. For this reason the good and excellent one, bearing in mind who he is, and whence he has come, and by whom he was created, focuses his attention on this and this only, how he may fill his place in an orderly fashion, and with due obedience to the god. (3.24.94–5) And again he repeats, 'I came into the world when it so pleased him, and I leave it again at his pleasure, and while I live this was my function – to sing hymns of praise to the god, to myself and to others, be it to one or to many' (3.26.30).

These passages on divine providence could serve to reinforce the argument for reason as our true nature for a theist.[29] Yet such providential considerations could not serve as a basis for this argument for an atheist who does not see the evolution of species, the time, place, and social condition of one's birth, etc., as guided by some kind of divine, overarching, cosmic intention.

For Epictetus, nevertheless, our function is to understand the universe and to do our best to interpret what its plan for us is (3.24.35).[30] We can try to maintain its harmonious order by, among other things, cheerfully carrying out that plan, being serene, unhampered, and unhindered (4.4.22), and praising the providence of it all. It is designed for good and success, not evil and failure. 'Just as a mark is not set up in order to be missed, so neither does the nature of evil arise in the universe' (*Ench.* 27).

C. Why the life of reason is a life of virtue

We have seen how the Stoics use their doctrine of *oikeiōsis* to argue that the final end, *eudaimonia*, consists in living and acting according to nature, and that for human beings this means living and acting according to reason. For Epictetus this means keeping oneself, one's *prohairesis*, in the proper, healthy state. But what has not yet been shown is why this certain state of the *prohairesis* must be one possessed of the traditional virtues (*aretai*), why this rational, healthy condition of the self must be the morally virtuous condition of the self.

Why be interested in the good? Epictetus argues that the good, by its very nature, is irresistible.

When the good appears it immediately attracts the soul to itself, while the evil repels the soul from itself. A soul will never refuse a clear impression of good, any more than the coinage of Caesar. On this hangs every impulse to act both of human and of god. That is why the good is preferred above every form of kinship. My father is nothing to me, but only the good. 'Are you so hard-hearted?' Yes, that is my nature. This is the coinage god has given to me. For that reason, if the good is something different from the noble and the just, then father and brother and country and all practices (*pragmata*) disappear. But shall I neglect my good, so that you may have it, and shall I make way for you? What for? 'I am your father.' But not a good. 'I am your brother.' But not a good. If, however, we locate the good in right volition, then the mere preservation of the relationships of life becomes a good ... (3.3.4–8; cf. 4.5.30–2)

To be attracted to the good is to value the health of the self. But the health of the self, on Epictetus' view, consists in valuing and incorporating the virtues of fidelity, self-respect, forbearance, benevolence, cooperation, etc. The individual judges what is good for her to be what is good for her volition. What is good for the *prohairesis* will be correct judgements. The correct judgements are the ones that strengthen and augment[31] one's natural affection (see Chapter 3), kindness, etc. If, however, one places one's good anywhere other than with the virtuous norms of oneself, then none of these virtues, nor the conduct that stems from them, can be in one's interest. One will of necessity not be inclined to them.

Obviously this account is incompatible with Epicureanism. For the Epicurean, psychic health is the absence of pain; the steady, pleasant disposition of the mind is the good. For the Stoic, in contrast, the good is not the pain-free, it is the noble. The virtuous fulfillment of all her familial, social, and civic roles is the demonstrative consequence of the Stoic locating the good with nobility, righteousness, justice and what is honorable.

If we understand the good to be right volition instead of pleasure, Epictetus argues, then respect for the relationships of life becomes mandatory, since only on this condition can one's volition be right. The good, the righteous, the honorable, the noble, and the just are properly judged to be co-extensive. If the good is interpreted to be anything other than this, then volition will inevitably be directed to the wrong (i.e. unhealthy, malevolent) goal. Epictetus staunchly believes that when human character is in accord with nature it is completely benevolent and devoid of vicious impulses.[32]

Now we can see more clearly how it is that the nature of the rational being is constituted so as to attain nothing of its own proper goods without contributing to the common interest (1.19.13). It is because, on the Stoic conception, it is simply human nature to perform virtuously one's civic roles and act so as to fulfill one's place in the community into which one is 'born and enrolled as a citizen' (2.23.39). The individual attains her *own* proper good as a *human being* exactly by also working for the good of others. Bonhöffer writes of Epictetus:

> Working for the welfare of one's fellow-being is to him therefore not a merely accidental or optional piece of morality, but the indispensable condition for attaining one's own happiness. As God cannot do otherwise than to be useful and do good, so the impulse for that purpose lies also in human nature, just because it is rational: for everything rational and good is at the same time useful.[33]

Epictetus thinks it defies nature's plan for a human being to luxuriate alone in a posh resort far from one's family and community (3.23.38). To forget this is exactly to forget oneself. This is why he urges that 'we must remember who we are, and what is our designation, and must endeavour to direct our actions, in the performance of our proper deeds (*ta kathēkonta*), to meet the capacities (*dunameis*) of our relationships' (4.12.16). We must remember our 'designation' (*onoma*) because it denotes our role. Epictetus elaborates on the nature of a role or 'profession' in this next passage:

> What, then, is the profession (*epangelia*) of a citizen? To treat nothing as a matter of private profit, not to plan about anything as though he were without community (*apoluton*), but to act like the foot or the hand, which, if they were rational and understood the natural constitution, would never exercise choice or desire in any other way but by reference to the whole (2.10.4).

The citizen is a member of a community, and so as a part should direct her actions toward the welfare of the whole. One of the individual's *onomata* is 'citizen'; she finds herself situated in that role, so she must play that role to the best of her ability.

Being a citizen, however, is not one's only role. Epictetus continues:

> Next remember this, that you are a son. What is the profession of this role (*prosōpon*)? To treat everything that is his own as belonging to his father, to be obedient to him in all things, never to badmouth him to anyone else, nor to say or do anything that will harm him, to give way to him in everything and yield him precedence, helping him as far as is within his power. Next know that you are also a brother. Upon this role also there is incumbent deference, obedience, courteous speech, never to claim against your brother any extra-volitional things, but cheerfully to give them up, so that in the volitional things you may have the best of it. For see what it is, at the price of a head of lettuce, if it so chance, or of a seat, for you to acquire his goodwill – how greatly you get the best of it there! Next, if you sit in the town council of some city, remember that you are a councillor; if you are young, remember that you are young; if old, that you are an elder; if a father, that you are a father. For each of these designations, when duly considered, always suggests the appropriate acts (*oikeia erga*). (2.10.7–11)

Each family relation (son, brother, father, husband) and each social role (citizen, councillor, youth, elder) has its own designation (*onoma*) and its own special role (*prosōpon*), and with these things each carries its own proper functions (*kathēkonta*). Epictetus does not consider the possibility of a conflict of duties. He thinks one need only consider what each *onoma* means in order to discover the conduct befitting to it.

> Our proper functions (*ta kathēkonta*) are in general measured by our relationships. He is a father. One is called upon to take care of him, to give way to him in all things, to submit when he reviles or strikes you. 'But he is a bad father.' Did nature,

then, relate *(oikeiōthēs)* you to a *good* father? No, but simply to
a father. 'My brother wrongs me.' Okay, then, maintain the
relation that you have toward him; and do not consider what
he is doing, but what you will have to do, if your volition is to
be in a state in accord with nature. ... In this way, therefore,
you will discover what proper function *(to kathēkon)* to expect
of your neighbour, your citizen, your commanding officer, if
you acquire the habit of looking at your relations with them.
(Ench. 30)

Mere reflection upon the relation one stands in toward another
automatically suggests the proper behavior for that relationship.
One must remember that who one is is substantially defined by the
roles one has. One must act in a sisterly way toward one's sister, in a
motherly way toward one's child, and so on in order to harmonize
with nature. As long as one behaves virtuously toward others, one
harmonizes with the normative goal of one's human nature, and
that is all that is of concern.

But does this constitute an explicit, rigorous argument for why
the conventional moral virtues, and not the vices, are rational
for human beings? Epictetus does not directly advance such an
argument. In one passage he appeals to our moral intuition. He
asserts that each creature is beautiful *(kalon)* when it achieves
supreme excellence in terms of its own nature (in sense 3 above).
Each creature has a different nature, hence each is beautiful in a
different way (3.1.3). Then, when he asks what excellence *(aretē)*
characterizes and makes beautiful a human being, he appeals to his
interlocutor:

Look at those who you yourself praise, when you praise people
dispassionately; is it the just, or the unjust? – The just. – Is it the
temperate, or the dissolute? – The temperate. – And is it the
self-controlled, or the uncontrolled? – The self-controlled. – In
making yourself that kind of person, therefore, rest assured that
you will be making yourself beautiful; but so long as you neglect
these things, you will necessarily be ugly, even if you use every
device to make yourself appear beautiful. (3.1.6–9)

Here Epictetus presupposes the pre-theoretical definition of the virtues in Aristotle's *Nicomachean Ethics* (i 13) as the traits that are praised. But why, we should challenge, praise the virtuous instead of the vicious? One could argue here from the *consensus omnium*: universal praise is a mark of the naturalness of the virtues as *oikeiōsis* is of the rational nature of humankind; *oikeiōsis* here could takes the place of Aristotle's notion of realizing one's potential.

This would fail to satisfy rugged non-traditionalists like Callicles, Thrasymachus, and Nietzsche, who do not subscribe to a conformist morality. Why is it in accord with nature and reason to have these social 'virtues' (conducive to herd mentality) instead of their opposite 'vices'? Even were we to grant Epictetus that *eudaimonia* is an inner state of calm and unperturbedness, why would we fail to attain the good by containing our desires to the evil wishes of the *prohairesis*? After all, we can imagine someone deriving enduring satisfaction from malicious thoughts of revenge upon an enemy. To stand Kant on his head, what precludes the good in itself for Epictetus from being *ill* will?

Korsgaard would seem to say that such a delicious malicious intent would in fact erode our mental health and be more self-destructive than self-satisfying.

> [W]e can agree that there are desires that conflict with one's health or happiness or that are self-destructive or pathological or simply burdensome out of all proportion to any gratification their fulfillment can provide. This already shows that the existence of a desire is not by itself a sufficient reason for the realization of its object; further conditions exist.[34]

On the Stoic account, these conditions are described in terms of the developmental parameters of 'appropriation' (*oikeiōsis*) to be presented below. So

> ... when we inquire into the basis for calling certain properties of a thing its 'virtues', we always come back to something that is relative to certain conditions of human life. It is our interests and

the bases of our interests that make certain qualities *virtues;* so these facts cannot make goodness a nonrelational attribute.[35]

We have sketched an explanation of what our interests are according to the (largely traditional) Stoic arguments – that is, why the social virtues are rational for us. Now we shall try to trace out what the bases for those interests are. In other words, the question now is: why must the right, healthy condition of the self be the one possessed of the social virtues instead of egoism and self-preservation narrowly understood?

While the argument I offer below appears nowhere in the *Diatribae,* Epictetus' remarks come close to suggesting it.[36] In any case, it is consistent with traditional Stoic doctrines. Striker writes:

> ... in order to show that nature prescribes virtuous behaviour, the Stoics would have to show that such behaviour is natural for man. And this is, I think, what they tried to do with their second appeal to *oikeiōsis,* thus making it the foundation of justice, and indeed of the other virtues as well. They point to the natural love of parents for their children, to the fact that man has been made by nature so as to procreate children, which means that nature must also have given him an impulse to care for their well-being (cf. Cic. *de Fin.* iii 62), and to an alleged fellow feeling of every human being for every other *qua* human being, in order to demonstrate that altruistic behaviour is natural for man, and therefore something nature has prescribed for him. The process of *oikeiōsis* to others is apparently supported by reasoning, which shows us that we are made to live in communities, and that the attitudes of care and respect should be extended to comprise not only our family and friends, but mankind in general.[37]

The first impulse of every human being is for self-preservation. This is the operation of the first kind of *oikeiōsis.* As human children mature into adolescents, their instinct to procreate manifests itself. Sexual reproduction becomes a secondary impulse of every human being. Then, having mated and conceived, human parents instinctively care for and nurture their newborn offspring. Upon the dawn of reason something like a Gestalt-shift occurs. Once our rational nature is achieved (at age 14), a different kind of *oikeiōsis* is activated that transforms for ever how we conceive of the world. The care, concern, and love for one's own children is generalized beyond one's family and friends to encompass all one's fellow-citizens. The concern for others is then generalized still further to include all members of humanity in virtue of their common possession of *logos*. Mutual affection becomes kindness, which turns into camaraderie. Camaraderie blossoms into fellowship, cooperation, general philanthropy, and concern for justice. As rationality develops into fullness, the pre-rational sentiments become affirmed and validated as rational virtues that preserve solidarity and cohesion within the human community. Without the social virtues, communal living and social interdependence would be impossible.

One could object that the Stoic does not in fact value interdependence at all since she intentionally insulates her mental states from the emotional network of the people around her. Isn't her art of living deliberately detached from her community?

This objection can be met by distinguishing two levels of interdependence. The Stoic does not give up her sense of solidarity with others since she does participate and cooperate with others in her living. The *prohairesis* the Stoic trains into the proper state is the one that *does* in fact seek interdependent social involvements. Her autonomy would be guaranteed only by recognizing her interdependence with others in this sense. So it would be in keeping with Stoic doctrine to value interdependence as part of the good life at this level *without* valuing external contingencies of luck. The Stoic would not permit her happiness to depend upon the contingent, often fragile, states of her communal associations.

The healthy soul, in acting virtuously toward others, promotes their survival and flourishing, and in so doing promotes its own survival and flourishing. Thus reason shows us that altruism is healthy.

When a man comes to reason, he will self-reflexively notice that he has been caring all along for other beings (for their sake) because he has seen them as belonging to himself: they were his offspring or his associates. But now he also comes to see himself as rational with the consequence that whatever else is rational will belong to him and be his just as much as, nay even more than, his offspring or other associates. So his basic other-regarding attitude of care (for their own sake) for others who were seen to belong to him must needs be extended to cover all rational beings. *They* are now seen to belong to him to the highest degree since in so far as they partake in rationality, which is common to them all, they are identical with him on the point which has by far the most important role to play for determining *what he himself is* (i.e. for determining his 'constitution' as we know it from Cicero, *Fin.* III 16). Thus the Stoics can speak in a very Kantian way of a 'city' of men and gods and connect the fact that each of us is a member of that city with a utilitarian type of altruism ... [38]

The commonality of *logos* in the universe as a whole includes the gods as well. Thus every rational being *qua* rational belongs to a single, comprehensive world-community. All rational beings are fellow-citizens of the universe.

To regard oneself as a strictly private individual separated from the rest of the community, with interests separate from those of its other members, Epictetus contends, is like regarding the foot as a thing detached from the body. It would be 'natural' for the person deliberately detached from the community to be totally selfish and value only her private wants and egotistic interests. Similarly, it would be 'natural' in this sense for the foot to be clean all the time. '[B]ut if you take it as a foot, and not as a thing detached, it will be appropriate for it to step into mud and trample on thorns and sometimes be cut off for the sake of the whole body; otherwise it will no longer be a foot. We ought to hold some such view also about ourselves' (2.5.24). We ought to take such a holistic, organic view of the situation of human beings in the world, according to Epictetus. If we detach ourselves from our community, we will no longer be human.[39] 'For what is a human being? A part of a state (*meros poleōs*) first of that state which is made up of gods and humans, and then of that which is said to be very close to the other, the state that is a small copy of the universal state' (2.5.26). All of nature, the entire universe (*kosmos*) is viewed as a state (*polis*) for the Stoic. Thus to separate oneself from this community is to separate one's human nature from Nature (sense 2) itself, and to deny the rationality inherent in both. This would be no less than to deny both the essence of oneself as a rational *kosmopolitēs* (citizen of the universe) and that of the universe itself; it would be to alienate oneself from one's own home, the *kosmos*.

We now have the theoretical justification for virtue as the content of a life according to reason. We can proceed to Epictetus' conception of *eudaimonia* as satisfaction with internals and how self-consciousness of one's own moral steadfastness liberates one into a state of spiritual serenity. Before turning to Epictetus' argument that *ataraxia* can be attained only by identifying the good with what is in my power, a few remarks on the meaning of 'happiness' are in order.

D. *Eudaimonia* and *ataraxia*

First of all, we must observe that although *eudaimonia* is customarily translated 'happiness,' the Greek concept is not exactly captured by this English word. For the ancient Greeks, *eudaimonia* is an enduring state, not a momentary success. It is not an occasional mood of contentment, a momentary lightness of spirit, or a feeling of pleasantness that can pass quickly, as 'happiness' sometimes connotes. Rather, an enduring, continuous, and relatively stable state of mind is what constitutes *eudaimonia*. Of course Epicurus, Zeno, and Pyrrho disagreed about what produced that state of mind.[40]

Epictetus operates with this same basic concept of *eudaimonia*, yet in some passages he also seems to be inclined to identify *eudaimonia* with *ataraxia* (unperturbedness).[41] For Seneca, Cicero, and the Stoics' rivals, the Epicureans and Skeptics, if one possesses mental peace and serenity, then one stands in need of nothing else. This is also reflected in Epictetus' conception of *eudaimonia*. For Epictetus this psychic calm results from not yielding to the upsetting, pathological judgements of the *prohairesis* (e.g. that certain externals are evil) called the *pathē* (passions).[42] For him, to be happy is to lack nothing. 'I do not yield to anger, or sorrow, or envy; I am not subject to restraint, or to compulsion. What do I yet lack? I enjoy leisure, I have peace of mind (*hēsuchia*)' (3.2.16). If one maintains this mental composure and self-control, Epictetus reasons, then one simply does not need anything else above and beyond that.

> If you are maintaining the character of passionlessness (*apathē*), of imperturbability, of tranquillity, if you are observing what happens rather than being yourself observed, if you are not envying those who are preferred in honor above you, if the mere subject matter of actions does not dazzle you, what do you lack? (4.4.9–10)

The person who is truly *eudaimōn* lacks nothing, needs nothing, is fully self-sufficient, and secures this self-sufficiency by maintaining the proper Stoic judgements.

> If you have these thoughts always at hand and rehearse them again and again in your own mind, and keep them in readiness, you will never need consoling, or strengthening. For shame is not having nothing to eat, but not having reason securing you against fear and against grief. (3.24.115–16)

To suffer from a deficiency of disciplined reason (*logos*) that causes one fear and grief[43] is a deficiency one is responsible for, and so it warrants disgrace. In contrast, a lack of food, which typically is a deficiency one is not responsible for causing, is nothing to be ashamed of, according to Epictetus.

But what if one actually values needing the support of others and considers interdependency as a good thing?[44] Earlier I explained Epictetus' account of the irrationality of choosing to be vulnerable and letting one's well-being rest upon insecure grounds, in Chapters 1 and 2. Here *autarkeia*, self-sufficient autonomy, directly opposes depending on others for one's happiness. For him this would amount to a desire for and enjoyment of risk via reliance on external contingencies. What is to be gained by (irrationally) risking one's happiness?

Longing for something or someone absent Epictetus considers to be another case of deficiency of reason that is incompatible with *eudaimonia*. 'But it is impossible that happiness, and yearning for what is not present, should ever be united. For happiness must already have all that it wants; it must resemble someone replete: he cannot feel thirst or hunger' (3.24.17). To thirst is to lack drink; to hunger is to lack food; to yearn is to lack the possession or presence of a thing. All of these are states of incompleteness. Most crucially, *psychic* incompleteness is directly contrary to the replete *autarkeia* characteristic of true happiness. This is certainly not to say that if the sage is hungry or thirsty she is unhappy (*kakodaimōn*). The true Stoic lacks nothing she takes to be good. Therefore, since food, drink, and physical comforts[45] are indifferents lying outside her *prohairesis*, lacking them cannot detract from her *eudaimonia*.

But why must happiness be this satisfaction with internals? In Chapter 1, I observed that we can easily imagine a shrewd capitalist who excels at amassing externals. Let us call this person Trump. Trump has tremendous desires for externals. He is greedy for vast material assets. He craves awesome political power. He has a fiendish lust for sex. He has an appetite for the most sumptuous food and wine money can buy. He loves the finest, most elegant clothes. He refuses to settle for less than the most luxurious furnishings. He adores the most glamorous and expensive cars, jets, and yachts in the world. Now, what if by some amazing boon Trump manages to acquire all these opulent externals, meets with uncanny political success, has ecstatically gratifying sex whenever he wants, and can buy whatever his little heart desires, on the slightest whim, at the snap of his credit card? Surely such a lucky person would be happy as long as his desires continue to be satisfied moment by moment and he can continue to do whatever he pleases. 'For what is it that every person is seeking? To live securely, to be happy, to do everything as he wishes to do, not to be hindered, not to be subject to compulsion' (4.1.46). As long as Trump gets every external he wants and successfully avoids all externals he fears, why would he fail to be *eudaimōn*? Why wouldn't Trump be the model of the perfectly happy sage instead of Socrates?

The answer, I believe, is that Trump does fear some externals in judging them to be evils. Not encountering them does not eliminate the fact that he does live in fear. No external contingencies, even if by his wildest fantasy they are repeatedly fortunate, will make Trump's internal state of character suffice for him. Trump, as long as his streak of good luck continues, experiences instant after instant of gratification. But since he does not desire and pursue what he truly *needs*, that is, steadfastness, his thinking in accord with nature (judging possession of the virtues to suffice for him), and an unvexed spirit (3.9.17), he will never be satisfied with the externals he gets. Nevertheless, one could reasonably object, if he gets what he wants every time, then by a process of induction won't he come to feel confident that his Midas touch will never fail? If this were to be the case, as improbable as it would be, it is likely that his unending string of external successes would after a while come to produce ennui instead of gratification.[46] But perhaps Trump would not grow bored of his fleeting, material glories even though he lacks unified moral and mental integrity, self-disciplined mastery of his desires, and self-sufficient psychic serenity.

Epictetus' conviction about Trump would be, as I mentioned above, that he *would* in fact be living in fear of losing his prized possessions. His material riches are by their very nature contingent and external to his *prohairesis* (self), and so are not essentially his. Thus Trump is wrong to consider them reliable. Epictetus addresses people who pursue externals as Trump does as follows: 'You have left the true path and are going off upon another; you are looking for serenity and happiness in the wrong place, where it does not exist, and you do not believe when another points them out to you. Why do you look for it outside?' (3.22.26–7). He goes on to show that it does not reside in the body, in possessions, in prestigious offices, or in royalty, since if it did,[47] nobody who had these things would be unhappy (3.22.27–30). But since these externally well-off people *are* unhappy, what is wrong with them?

You have neglected and ruined whatever that is in you by which we desire, avoid, choose, and refuse. Neglected how? It remains ignorant of the reality (*ousia*) of the good, to which it was born, and of the evil, and of what is its own private possession, and what is alien to it. (3.22.31–2)

Trump would act in ignorance of these things until he is thwarted, just once, in one of his material ventures. Then, were he to reflect, he could grasp the Stoic insight that his true self is his own volition, his assent, his choices, refusals, decisions, intentions, beliefs, judgements, and valuations. Trump is deaf to Zeus' words: '"Behold," says he, "your fears are at haphazard, it is in vain that you desire what you desire. Do not look for your goods outside, but look for them within yourselves; otherwise you will not find them"' (3.24.112). Trump should not be surprised that since it is his *prohairesis* that is his real self, and in reality its judgements (*dogmata*) are the only things that, being inseparable from him, truly belong to him, happiness is to be found within himself and it cannot be extracted from externals.

Trump would continue to be a slave to externals as long as he pursued his good in them instead of in himself. Trump could not be happy on Epictetus' conception of happiness as freedom.

At this time is freedom anything but the right to live as we want? 'Nothing else.' Tell me, then, people, do you want to live in error? 'We do not.' Well, no one living in error is free. Do you want to live in fear, in sorrow, in turmoil? 'By no means.' Well then, nobody in fear, or sorrow, or turmoil, is free, but whoever is rid of sorrows and fears and turmoils, this one is by the same route also rid of slavery. (2.1.23–4)

Trump would still be under the compulsion of the tax authorities of course, but even were the President himself to be under his thumb, Trump would still always be subject to earthly phenomena and circumstance.

Can he [Caesar], then, at all provide us with peace from fever too, and from shipwreck too, and from fire, or earthquake, or lightning? Come, can he give us peace from erotic love? He cannot. From sorrow? From envy? He cannot, from absolutely none of these things. But the doctrine of the philosophers promises to give us peace from these troubles too. And what does it say? 'People, if you heed me, wherever you may be, whatever you may be doing, you will feel no pain, no anger, no compulsion, no hindrance, but you will pass your lives in tranquillity and in freedom from every disturbance.' (3.13.10–11)

But isn't Trump free as long as his streak of luck lasts, as long as he avoids fever, helicopter crashes, IRS tax audits, etc.? 'Since he is free for whom all things happen according to his volition, and whom none can restrain' (1.12.9), if all externals go his way by satisfying his wants, then how would Trump be restrained? Though he may dodge the tax audit this year, he may still worry about it in the future *unless* he has total confidence in the cunning of his tax attorneys. Though his corporations currently return great profits, the fear of hostile takeovers *may* still weigh on his mind. On the other hand, the possibility that Carl Icahn could take him on might actually excite Trump if he is cocksure of his superiority.

Epictetus would only presuppose the Stoic view here by replying that Trump is wrong to be self-confident in regard to things external to him. Epictetus would assert that Trump's attachment to the grandeur of Trump Tower and his Taj Mahal will not give him tranquillity: '"Athens is beautiful." But happiness is much more beautiful, tranquillity, freedom from turmoil, having your own affairs under no one's control' (4.4.36). In placing his concern in externals, Trump is necessarily subjecting his affairs to factors beyond his control: the stock market, Carl Icahn, the weather, etc. Externals are ultimately under Zeus' control, yet Trump would not acknowledge anything of this sort since everything he cares about goes his way. 'For the sake of what is called freedom some hang themselves, others jump over precipices, sometimes whole cities are destroyed; for true freedom, which cannot be plotted against and is secure, will you not yield to god, upon demand, what he has given?' (4.1.171–2). Trump does not have true freedom, that is, the freedom of will which, among other things, accepts all that happens, i.e. follows god's will (cf. 4.3.9). Trump wants to have Nature's events conform to his will; and, as long as his incredible good fortune lasts, he will believe that it does. For those of us who are not born under Trump's most improbably lucky star, however, we need to conform our will to Nature in sense 2. Epictetus' diviner proclaims: 'If you will (*theleis*), you are free; if you will, you will not have to blame anyone, or complain about anyone; all will be in accordance with not only your will (*gnomēn tēn sēn*), but at the same time the god's' (1.17.28). Trump wills the wrong things, and so is not free.

The goal of Stoicism according to Epictetus is: 'to learn how to get rid of pain, and turmoil, and humiliation, and so become free' (4.6.8). Pride in material successes is not justified since they are predominantly a matter of fortune. Mastery of 'the necessary principles, those that enable one, if he sets forth from them, to become free of grief, fearless, passionless, unhindered, and free' (4.6.16), on the other hand, is worthy of pride. Epictetus also directly attacks the Epicurean doctrine that pleasure (*hēdonē*) is the good.

> What subject has arisen that we wish to investigate? – Pleasure. – Submit it to the standard, toss it into the scales. Must the good be the sort of thing that we can properly have confidence and trust in? – It must. – Can we properly have confidence, then, in something insecure? – No. – Pleasure is not something secure, is it? – No. – Away with it, then, and eject it from the scales, and drive it far away from the region of good things. (2.11.19–21)

Not just any internal state can be the good; it must be secure and reliable.

Freedom from humiliation, frustration, anxiety, disappointment, worry, fear, sorrow, grief, misery, anger, envy, jealousy, spite, loss, mistaken assent, erroneous judgement, failure, hindrance, subjection to others, and the contingency of fortune – freedom from all these disturbances is for Epictetus' interlocutor the greatest good. 'Does freedom seem to you to be a good? – The greatest. – Is it possible, then, for someone who has this greatest good to be unhappy or to fare badly? – No. – Whoever, therefore, you see to be unhappy, miserable, grieving, confidently declare not to be free' (4.1.52). The Stoic's freedom is absolute because her true self, secure in its moral steadfastness, simply cannot fare badly. Trump's self, which is directed toward external items instead of virtues, is insecure and precarious.

Trump follows the reasoning of the progressor (*prokoptōn*) this far, that '... desire is for good things and aversion is toward bad things, and having also learned that serenity and calm (*euroun kai apathes*) are only attained by a person if he succeeds in getting what he desires and avoids what he is averse to ...' (1.4.1) but it is the next move that Trump does not make because of his incredibly good fortune with externals:

> ... such a person has utterly eliminated from himself desire, or else postponed it to another time, and feels aversion only toward volitional things (*ta prohairetika*). For if he avoids anything that is not volitional, he knows that he will sometimes encounter something despite his aversion to it, and be unfortunate. (1.4.1–2)

Epictetus does not countenance the possibility that there could be someone like Trump who has so fully glutted his ravenous appetites for externals that he would stand in no need of virtue. It is firm possession of virtue in the form of correct ethical judgements on which an agent can always rely. Our philosopher never doubts for an instant that virtue, or rather, as I will suggest, awareness and appreciation *of* one's own virtue, produces happiness and serenity: 'Now if virtue (*aretē*) promises to create happiness and calmness and serenity, then certainly progress toward virtue is progress toward each of these' (1.4.3). But why should we believe that *aretē* by itself has the power to produce the state of mind of serene *eudaimonia*? Can't an agent know she is virtuous yet be depressed and miserable nonetheless?

Such a grief-stricken moral agent fails to appreciate that she has the goods of the soul and that they matter much more than adequate food, housing, health care and a decent job. Virtue is its own joyous reward for the Stoic. But why should one not despair of ever being *eudaimōn* since, unlike Trump, the rest of us inevitably have our desires for externals thwarted?

Just because we cannot reasonably expect to gratify our desires if we allow them to extend beyond what is in our control, Epictetus refuses to concede that *eudaimonia* is for that reason unattainable. We ought not to despair over the loss of externals because externals simply do not and cannot compare in value to the goods of the soul, i.e. internals, the virtues.

> Keep this at hand whenever you lose any external thing: What are you getting for it? And if this is more valuable, never say, 'I have suffered a loss'; whether it is a horse for an ass, an ox for a sheep, a fine deed for a little money, peacefulness for futile discourse, and self-respect for filthy talk. If you remember this, you will everywhere maintain the kind of person (*prosōpon*) you are as it ought to be. If not, notice that your time is being spent in vain, and the trouble you are now taking for yourself will all be upset and spill out wasted. Little is needed to ruin and upset everything, just a slight aberration from reason. For the helmsman to capsize his ship he does not need the same preparation as he does to keep it safe, but if he turns it a little too far into the wind, he is lost; and even if he does not do it deliberately, but merely loses his concentration momentarily, he is lost. Here it is like that too; if you doze just for a moment, all that you have gained up till then is gone. Attend, therefore, your impressions (*phantasiai*), and watch over them sleeplessly. For it is no small matter that you are guarding, but self-respect, and fidelity, and constancy, passionlessness (*apatheia*), painlessness, fearlessness, imperturbability; in short, freedom. (4.3.1–7)

The level of *askēsis* – systematic training in self-discipline – that is demanded by Epictetus in this quotation is extraordinary. Even the briefest slouching from the vigilance of reason endangers one's tranquillity. On the basis of this passage it seems safe to infer that Epictetus does share the assessment of his interlocutor at 4.1.52 that freedom is the greatest good. Epictetan freedom is neither blindness to nor disregard for the suffering of others. Rather, it is a single-minded, concerted effort to be noble, honorable, faithful, kind, and good. The Stoic strives to be ever vigilant in working to achieve virtue and, through the rigorous exercise of rationality, to be free from vice. Nothing matters more to her.

E. The strength of Stoicism

Before discussing what strike me as the most compelling ideas of Epictetus' ethical thought, I must identify three serious weaknesses.

The first arises from his dualistic ontology. With this doctrine he is squarely in line with the rest of the Stoa, which maintained a dualistic ontology of an active, formal principle (*nous/logos* = intellect/reason), and a corresponding passive, inferior principle (*hulē* = matter). The problem this ontology creates for Epictetus is that although he greatly downplays the active power that the health of one's body has on the functioning of one's cognitive processes,[48] there is certainly no denying the physiological basis of many or all mental disorders and cognitive dysfunctions. Stockdale reports that he and his fellow POWs '... found that over the course of time our minds had a tremendous capacity for invention and introspection, but had the weakness of being an integral part of our bodies,' and explains to a fellow POW his disappointment in having learned that Descartes was wrong, declaring that 'I had discovered that body and mind are inseparable.'[49] In Epictetus' defense one can say that on his account it is choiceworthy to keep our bodies in good working order. This can in many cases at least ameliorate the body's adverse effects on cognitive functions.

Moreover, although the *prohairesis* would seem to be either itself a physical entity, or else a kind of movement of the *hēgemonikon*, which is physical, the *prohairesis* somehow has the causal power to produce presumably non-physical judgements (*dogmata*), which function as the propositions (*lekta*, literally 'sayables') to which reason (*logos*) assents. It is not at all clear on the Stoic account how the physical intellect actually interacts with these non-physical *lekta* that 'subsist' but do not 'exist' as bodies do. The *hēgemonikon* and *psuchē* are, after all, bodily entities. In so far as they are bodily, however, they are subject to the rigid Stoic determinism governing all corporeal objects. But if the faculties that control one's behavior are determined by a cause (Zeus' providential will) or causes (the constitution of material things) beyond one's own control, then there is simply no room for moral accountability as we ordinarily understand it. Ethical responsibility seems to be precluded by the causal determinism of Stoic physics. I suggest that this problem in Stoic physics is what largely motivated Epictetus to develop his concept of the *prohairesis*. He makes total freedom essential to the *prohairesis* in his attempt to save moral responsibility from the complete physical determinism espoused by the Stoa. This is why volition receives so much emphasis in this original thinker of late Stoicism.[50]

The second weakness is more grave from an ethical perspective. His teleological view is thoroughly anthropocentric, and this leads him to hold the very popular belief that all animals are by nature for the use of humans. He repeats the idea that animals were born for our service at 1.6.18, 2.8.7, and at length at 1.16.1–8. On this doctrine too he follows the traditional Stoic doctrine that all non-human animals are non-rational. Some ancient Greeks, however, were mindful enough of the sentience of animals to advocate vegetarianism.[51] It is ironic that, as a Stoic, Epictetus defined the final end as 'living in accordance with nature,' yet he failed to see how exploiting non-human animals for our own interests without any concern for them ignores sentient beings' interest in avoiding pain and suffering. This view is known as speciesism. The speciesist holds that since we are human beings, we may legitimately use, abuse, and exploit all non-humans for the satisfaction of even our most trivial desires.

Epictetus was certainly on the right track in maintaining that it is our interpretive judgements (*dogmata*) of things and events that usher value into the world. 'If human beings have an intrinsic value by virtue of the capacity for valuing things, then human beings bring goodness into the world.'[52] Yet although Epictetus is quite cognizant of the intrinsic value of human persons in so far as that is where reason and the virtues are located, his ethical vision is too narrow to recognize the inherent interests of *all* sentient beings, human *and* non-human, rational, semi-rational, and non-rational.

Concerning broader environmental concerns, some ancient thinkers opposed appropriating minerals from the earth. 'Roman civilization was more pragmatic, secular, and commercial [than Greek civilization] and its environmental impact more intense. Yet Roman writers such as Ovid, Seneca, Pliny, and the Stoic philosophers openly deplored mining as an abuse of their mother, the earth.'[53] Interestingly, the Stoics not only personify but also engender the earth. But my point is that the mentality that sanctions the greedy exploitation and oppression of any and all sentient beings for the production and consumption of unnecessary and often unhealthy commodities is as rebarbative in Epictetus as it is elsewhere. Yet ecological consciousness is not, at least on conceptual if not on historical grounds, an implausible construal of the Stoic formulation of the final end.[54] Epictetus would, I contend, agree that it is not rational to damage or destroy natural environments as we routinely do.

The third salient weakness of Epictetus' ethics stems from his conservative political stance, which he shares with Aristotle, Cicero, and most ancients. His political quietism de-emphasizes the conscientious citizen's *kathēkon* of enacting social, economic, and political reform. Epictetus thinks Stoicism, unlike Epicureanism, promotes the stability of the state. Yet one could argue that although winter harmonizes with summer, poverty does not harmonize with wealth. Economic injustice and social oppression make for moral dissonance, not harmony. Either Epictetus does not perceive the authoritarian lethargy and inertia that perpetuate injustices of the status quo, or else he has no interest in urging his pupils, young sons of Roman noblemen, to work for justice in the form of the *political* freedom of the disadvantaged.[55] Panaetius and Cicero stress the citizen's public, political *officia*, i.e. the dutiful execution of one's senatorial tasks. Epictetus' comparative silence on this score is somewhat ironic, in view of the central role assigned to the idea of *mental* freedom in his ethical system. He prefers to concentrate on the private liberation of the self (*prohairesis*) in a manner arguably akin to the Hindu idea of Moksha.

Nevertheless, Stoicism does at least latently contain the theoretical matrix for natural law theory in its concept of the *kosmopolitēs*, the 'citizen of the universe.' Julia Annas rightly recognizes that

> [t]he Stoics hold that normal ethical development will result in the agent's having equal concern for all humans just as humans, a remarkable insistence on the need for ethics to include an impartial point of view not paralleled in Aristotle or Epicurus. Familiarization with others thus is not complete until one gives oneself no more ethical weight in one's deliberations than "the remotest Mysian," as the hostile ancient commentator on the *Theaetetus* puts it. And this idea is quite unAristotelian.[56]

Aristotle is notorious for his defense of slavery in the *Politics*. In contrast, Stoicism harbors an ethical rationale which, were it carried out to its logical conclusion, would undercut the bigoted parochialism at the root of all forms of the insiders vs. outsiders mentality. Hence the 'citizen of the world' with a global ethical perspective would directly oppose oppression and unjust discrimination in all its forms, including nationalism, elitism, racism, sexism, homophobia, and speciesism.

In conclusion, I submit that the strength of Stoicism lies in the philosophical merits of a cogent, consistent, and powerfully articulated ethical system and moral psychology. It is these same ethical ideas which, due to their forceful content, both account for the influence Stoicism exercised on subsequent thinkers in the history of Western philosophy[57] and call for the attention and closer scrutiny of contemporary moral philosophers.[58] These ideas include: (1) the life-affirming judgement that we should manage the things within our power as best we can, and accept what is beyond our control on the conviction that it can be made to turn out for the best in the long run. This belief, habitually applied, produces a resilient and psychologically healthy optimism that conduces to coping tenaciously, and so very often successfully, with the affairs within our power; (2) the doctrine that happiness is 'up to us' and not contingent upon luck, since the excellence of a person is such that if one truly possessed moral integrity and a sound character, then one would thereby possess profound inner satisfaction and the noblest kind of happiness; (3) the idea that one can love another without making that love conditional upon its always, or ever, being reciprocated. This is the conviction that love is to be given freely in pure joy with no admixture of sorrow.

Perhaps such a beautifully expressed conception of happiness as the spiritual elation that results from being aware of one's own moral steadfastness, emotional freedom, and psychic integrity could only have been voiced by someone born a slave.

Notes

1. Stephen Morris has questioned why this intensity of mental discipline is desirable and not itself a kind of pathology. I think Epictetus' optimism about the ability of human beings to achieve enduring happiness is so strong that he views defeatism as a kind of pathology. However, relentness mental discipline is, to his mind, the only means to attain such happiness. Mental laziness defeats the possibility of progress.

2. In ancient Greek philosophy the idea of becoming like god goes back at least to Plato, and it plays an equally important role in his philosophy; see, for example, Armstrong (2004). Aristotle construes the human good, *eudaimonia*, as the activity of *theōria* (contemplation); we become like god through scientific theorizing, that is, understanding for the sake of understanding. The goal of achieving imperturbability (*ataraxia*) in the form of complete absence of pain and distress is the Epicureans' model of becoming like the gods. So the Stoics are rooted in a reputable philosophical tradition of setting up becoming like god as *the* normative target.

3. Stephen Morris suggested this to me.

4. I highlight 'for us' because it is important to remember that Socrates and Diogenes the Cynic are held up by Epictetus as individuals who very probably achieved sagehood. According

to the Stoics, the sage does not even perceive incorrectly. The sage's mind is organized so as never to assent to *phantasiai* of seeming-chairs, merely apparent tables and fake pens. The sage actually sees, hears, feels and in general senses the world in such a way as never to be deceived into taking a bogus book to be a real book. The sage always pictures the world correctly and infallibly.

5. For a full discussion of Epictetus' views on moral progress and perfection in comparison with those of other Stoics, see Bonhöffer (1894: 144–53).

6. This Nietzschean interpretation arose in conversation with Stephen Morris.

7. For the victim of torture it requires hardening the mind to the pains of the body.

8. I suspect that almost no one has the disposition of mind that judges itself happy with the possession of moral integrity alone and that could regard extended periods of bodily pain as indifferent.

9. Epictetus has what Fromm calls a 'rational faith' in his Stoicism: 'rational faith is rooted in an independent conviction based upon one's own productive observing and thinking, *in spite of* the majority's opinion' (Fromm, 1974: 103; his emphasis).

10. The historical Socrates was such a complex individual that his remoteness in time even from Epictetus' day may very well make him a problematic paradigm for the sage. Neatly separating his personal idiosyncrasies from his 'sagely essence' that we should emulate would be a very difficult, delicate task. For the pervasive influence of Plato's Socrates on Epictetus, see Long (2002).

11. But cf. *Ench.* 37: 'If you undertake a role (*ti prosōpon*) which is beyond your powers, you both disgrace yourself in that one, and at the same time neglect the role that you might have filled successfully.' Comparing these two texts, Epictetus evidently thinks that striving to have a character as excellent as that of Socrates, keeping his body fit, and managing his property prudently, are all roles *within* his power.

12. I borrow the following from Bonhöffer (1894: 13n).

13. Liddell *et al.* (1996: 1202).
14. Pembroke (1971: 116). See also Inwood (1996) and Blundell (1990).
15. Pembroke (1971: 116).
16. Striker (1983: 145).
17. Long and Sedley(1987: Vol. 1, 351).
18. Annas (1990: 82). She defends this choice on the grounds that, '[i]t does better than other English words in suggesting the idea of 'family' in *oikeios* as well as the idea of coming to belong, the opposite of *allotriōsis*, for which we do have an English equivalent, "alienation"' (1990: 94n).
19. Engberg-Pedersen (1986).
20. This phrase from Engberg-Pedersen (1986: 154) I take to mean a fact that is itself an evaluation.
21. *Ibid.*, 171.
22. Frede (1986: 109).
23. Striker (1983: 155).
24. *Ibid.*, 159.
25. Voelke (1973: 157); this is Bernard Reginster's translation of: 'Selon l'enseignement stoïcien, les vertus morales sont les mêmes pour tous, sans acception de sexe, ni de race, ni de condition sociale.'
26. Striker explains the Stoics' assumed identity between the 'life of reason' and the 'life in accordance with nature' like this: '... being guided by reason is the same as living in accordance with nature – that is, in conscious observation of nature's rules – because man has been given reason for the pursuit of truth; finding out truth amounts to discovering nature – universal nature as well as one's own, since everything there is, is part of universal nature; so being guided by reason means being guided by one's insight into nature' (Striker, 1983: 154).
27. See Chapter 2.
28. Bonhöffer enumerates a total of six different *telos* formulae at work in Epictetus:
    1. To follow God, to fill in the place assigned by Him, to adjust or respectively to submit one's own will to Him, to imitate Him, to maintain communion with Him. 2.

To recognize nature, to follow it, to live according to it. 3. To develop the soul (the *logos*, the *hēgemonikon*, the *prohairesis*, the *dianoia* and its particular functions: *orexis*, *hormē*, *sunkatathesis*) and to shape and preserve it correctly, i.e. according to nature and reason. 4. To maintain one's own (one's *prohairesis*) and to disregard the foreign, extra-prohairetic. 5. To keep one's *daimōn* unharmed, not to abandon one's *prosōpon*, one's moral honor and dignity. 6. To suffice unto oneself, To be free, dispassionate and sinless, steadfast and unshakable. (Bonhöffer, 1894: 12)

This is my translation of:

'1. Gott folgen, den von ihm angeweisenen Platz ausfüllen, ihm den eigenen Willen anpassen resp. unterwerfen, ihn nachahmen, mit ihm Gemeinschaft pflegen. 2. Die Natur erkennen, ihr folgen, ihr gemäss leben. 3. Die Seele (den Logos, das Hegemonikon, die Proairesis, die Dianoia und ihre einzelnen Funktionen: *orexis*, *hormē*, *sunkatathesis*) ausbilden und richtig, d.h. natur- und vernunftgemäss, gestalten und bewahren. 4. Das Eigene (die Proairesis) wahren und das Fremde, Aproairetische, lassen. 5. Den Dämon unverletzt erhalten, das Prosopon, die sittliche Ehre und Wurde, nicht preisgaben. 6. Such selbst genugen, frei, leidenschaftslos und sündlos, beständig und unerschütterlich sein.

29. Cf. Kant's preface to the *Grundlegung* and Hamlet's 'Sure he that made us with such large discourse, looking before and after, gave us not that capability and godlike reason to fust in us unused' (iv. 4, 36–9).

30. Without an accurate understanding of the *kosmos*, Epictetus does not seem to think that there is an intelligible context for properly understanding what we are, how we should shape our lives, how we should relate to others, or where we belong, both locally and globally.

31. As we shall see below, the circle of people who are the objects of one's affection, love, and concern is extended beyond one's family, friends, co-workers, compatriots, and even fellow-

travellers to encompass all who are fellow 'citizens of the universe.'

32. As we saw in Section C of Chapter 3, Epictetus believes loving concern for one's children and fellowship with others are inherent in human nature.

33. My translation of: 'Das Wirken zum Wohle des Nächsten ist ihm also nicht ein bloss accidentelles oder fakultatives Stück der Sittlichkeit, sondern die unerlässliche Bedingung für die Erlangung der eigenen Glückseligkeit. Wie Gott nicht anders kann, als nützen und wohltun, so liegt der Trieb dazu auch in der menschlichen Natur, eben weil sie vernünftig ist: denn alles Vernünftige und Gute ist zugleich Nutzen bringend' (Bonhöffer, 1894: 158–9).

34. Korsgaard (1983: 183).

35. *Ibid.*, 188; her emphasis.

36. Cf. 2.5.26; 3.7.20; the end of 3.24.49; 4.5.35; *Ench.* 24. 4–5.

37. Striker (1983: 163).

38. Engberg-Pedersen (1986: 176). To avoid anachronism, Kant's kingdom of ends should be described as echoing the Stoics' idea, rather than the other way around.

39. For a study emphasizing the familial, social, and communal elements of Roman Stoicism, see Reydams-Schils (2005).

40. For Aristotle *eudaimonia* describes a kind of activity of living, not a state of mind. This Aristotelian orientation does not, I believe, clash with the Stoic view that *eudaimonia* is intimately related to a certain art of living.

41. See, for example, Irwin (1986: esp. 224–8).

42. See the discussion of the *pathē* in Chapter 3.

43. If a person is outraged over social injustices and is infuriated by the humiliations and degradations of poverty, this person, on Epictetus' view, would be disturbing herself by means of her pathological judgements. Hatred, anger, and malevolence for *any* reason indicates an unhealthy, tormented soul. Epictetus' benevolent optimism is such that resentment and grief, even over the miserable material conditions that *others* suffer, is counterproductive since in itself it only succeeds in harming oneself. Action directed to alleviate the suffering of others

must be motivated by philanthropy and social responsibility dictated by the *kathēkonta*, if the soul is to be healthy. Detesting the people who are the cause of human suffering is, on the Stoic's positive-minded view, a self-mutilating motivation for social reform.

44. This question was raised in discussion with Sally Haslanger.
45. Hence one of the paradoxes of Stoicism: the sage is happy even on the rack.
46. I owe this insight to Ron Wilburn.
47. An Aristotelian would judge this Stoic inference to be faulty: if satisfaction of *every* desire for externals does not produce happiness, then happiness does not involve *at all* the satisfaction of any desire for externals. I owe this insight to Stephen Morris.
48. See 3.2.5, for example.
49. Stockdale (1978: 102). See also Sherman (2005). The Stoics were physicalists regarding the soul, holding that it is a mixture of fire and air (*pneuma*). They reasoned that: (1) the body and the soul act upon each other; (2) the body is physical; (3) therefore, the soul is physical. See Long and Sedley (1987: Vol. 1, 272–4).
50. 'It would, however, be a superficial and insufficient view to reduce Epictetus' thought to a summary and rigid intellectualism that would rest content with subordinating the will to knowledge. In fact, moral action such as he conceives it undeniably includes a strong volitional component' – Voelke (1973: 136). This is Bernard Reginster's translation of: 'Ce serait toutefois en rester à une vue superficielle et insuffisante que de réduire la pensée d'Épictète à un intellectualisme sommaire et rigide qui se contenterait de subordonner le vouloir au savoir. En fait, l'action morale telle qu'il la conçoit comporte indéniablement une forte composante volitive.'
51. Pythagoras, Empedocles, Theophrastus, Plutarch, Plotinus, and Porphyry are prominent examples of ancients who thought it wrong to eat animals; see Dombrowski (1984).
52. Korsgaard (1983: 195).
53. Merchant (1980: 3).

54. Cf. Cheney (1989). He sees the subtext underlying ancient Stoicism as importantly similar to the subtext underlying contemporary 'deep ecology.' Unfortunately he neglects actual Stoic texts in his zeal to diagnose the alienation he views as inherent in both Stoic philosophy and deep ecology as propounded by Warwick Fox, Bill Devall, George Sessions, and Arne Naess. *Contra* Cheney, the sensitive reader of Stoic texts can discern positive parallels between Stoic naturalism and sound social ecology as propounded by Murray Bookchin; see Stephens (1994).

55. See Stephens (1997).

56. Annas (1990: 91–2).

57. Most notably Spinoza and Kant, but see also Long (2002: 259–74).

58. Becker (1998) has done exactly that, evidently having been persuaded that 'the Stoics were onto something important in ethical theory – not just emotionally satisfying, but something that corresponds to some deeply rooted moral intuition in such a way that it should find its place in any ethical theory proper' (Engberg-Pedersen, 1986: 146).

Bibliography

Algra, K., van der Horst, P., and Runia, D. (1996) (eds), *Polyhistor: Studies in the History and Historiography of Ancient Philosophy.* Leiden: Brill.

Angers, J.-E. d' (1954), 'Sénèque, Épictète et le stoïcisme dans l'oeuvre de René Descartes', *Revue de Théologie et de Philosophie,* Sér. 3, année 4, 169–96.

Annas, J. (1990), 'The Hellenistic Version of Aristotle's Ethics', *Monist,* 73 (1), 80–96.

—— (1993), *The Morality of Happiness.* Oxford: Oxford University Press.

Armstrong, J. M. (2004), 'After the Ascent: Plato on Becoming Like God', *Oxford Studies in Ancient Philosophy,* 26 (Summer), 171–83.

Barnes, J. (1997), *Logic and the Imperial Stoa.* Leiden: Brill.

Barth, H. (1951), 'Die Bedeutung der Freiheit bei Epiktet und Augustin', in *Das Menschenbild im Lichte des Evangeliums; Festschrift zum 60. Geburtstag von ... Emil Brunner.* Zürich: Zwingli-Verlag, pp. 49–64.

Becker, L. (1998), *A New Stoicism.* Princeton: Princeton University Press.

Billerbeck, M. (1978), *Epiktet: von Kynismus* (Philosophia Antiqua Vol. 34). Leiden: Brill.

—— (1996), 'The Ideal Cynic from Epictetus to Julian', in Branham and Goulet-Cazé, (1996) pp. 205–21.

Blundell, M. W. (1990), 'Parental Nature and Stoic *Oikeiosis*', *Ancient Philosophy,* 10 (Fall), 221–42.

Bodson, A. (1967), *La Morale sociale des derniers Stoïciens, Sénèque, Épictète et Marc Aurèle.* Paris: Société d'Édition 'Les Belles Lettres'.

Bonforte, J. (1955), *The Philosophy of Epictetus.* New York: Philosophical Library.

162   *Stoic Ethics*

Bonhöffer, A. (1890), *Epictet und die Stoa*. Stuttgart: Enke.
—— (1894), *Die Ethik des Stoikers Epictet*. Stuttgart: Enke.
—— (1911), *Epiktet und das Neue Testament*. Giessen: Töpelmann.
Bosshard, E. (1929), 'Épictète', *Revue de Théologie et de Philosophie*, 72 (Études sur le stoïcisme dans l'antiquité), 202–16.
Boter, G. (1999), *The Encheiridion of Epictetus and Its Three Christian Adaptations*. Leiden and Boston: Brill.
Branham, R. B. and Goulet-Cazé, M.-O. (1996), *The Cynics: The Cynic Movement in Antiquity and Its Legacy*. Berkeley: University of California Press.
Brennan, T. (2005), *The Stoic Life: Emotions, Duties, and Fate*. Oxford: Oxford University Press.
Brunt, P. A. (1977), 'From Epictetus to Arrian', *Athenaeum*, 55, 19–48.
Cadou, R. G. (1954), 'Épictète et Galien', *Bulletin de l'Association Guillaume Budé* (Lettres d'humanité 13), 94–101.
Capelle, W. (1948), *Epiktet, Teles und Musonius: Wege zu glückseligem Leben*. Zürich: Artemis-Verlag.
Cheney, J. (1989), 'The Neo-Stoicism of Radical Environmentalism', *Environmental Ethics*, 11 (4), 293–325.
Cizek, E. (1975), 'Épictète et l'heritage stocïen', *Studii Clasice*, XVII, 71–87.
Colardeau, Th. (1903), *Étude sur Épictète*. Paris: A. Fontemoing.
Cooper, J. M. (1989), 'Greek Philosophers on Euthanasia and Suicide', in B. A. Brody (ed.), *Suicide and Euthanasia: Historical and Contemporary Themes*. Dordrecht and Boston: Kluwer Academic Publishers, pp. 24–9.
De Lacy, P. (1943), 'The Logical Structure of the Ethics of Epictetus', *Classical Philology*, 38, 112–25.
Decleva Caizzi, F. (1977), 'La tradizione antistenico-cinica in Epitteto', in G. Giannantoni (ed.), *Scuole socratiche minori e filosofia ellenistica*. (Pubblicazioni del Centro di studio per la storia della storiografia filos., 4). Bologna: il Mulino, pp. 93–113.
Dillon, J. M. and Long, A. A. (1988) (eds), *The Question of 'Eclecticism': Studies in Later Greek Philosophy*. Berkeley: University of California Press.

Dobbin, R. (1991), 'Προαίρεσις in Epictetus', *Ancient Philosophy*, 11 (Spring), 111–35.

—— (1998), *Epictetus: Discourses Book I*, tr. and commentary. Oxford: Oxford University Press.

Dombrowski, D. A. (1984), *The Philosophy of Vegetarianism*. Amherst: University of Massachusetts Press.

Döring, K. (1974), 'Sokrates bei Epiktet', in H. Gundert, K. Döring, and W. Kullmann (eds), *Studia Platonica: Festschrift für Hermann Gundert zu seinem 65. Geburtstag*. Amsterdam: Grüner, pp. 195–226.

Dragona-Monachou, M. (1978–79), 'Prohairesis in Aristotle and Epictetus: A Comparison with the Concept of Intention in the Philosophy of Action', Φιλοσοφία, 8–9, 265–308.

Dudley, D. R. (1967), *A History of Cynicism: From Diogenes to the 6th century A.D.* Hildesheim: G. Olms.

Edelstein, L. (1966), *The Meaning of Stoicism*. London: Oxford University Press.

Engberg-Pedersen, T. (1986), 'Discovering the Good: *Oikeiosis* and *Kathekonta* in Stoic Ethics', in Schofield and Striker (1986), pp. 145–83.

Frankl, V. E. (1962), *Man's Search for Meaning*. Boston: Beacon Press.

Frede, M. (1986), 'The Stoic Doctrine of the Affections of the Soul', in Schofield and Striker (1986), pp. 93–110.

Fromm, E. (1974), *The Art of Loving*. New York: Harper & Row.

Germain, G. (1964), *Épictète et la spiritualité stoïcienne*. Paris: Éditions du Seuil.

Graver, M. (2003), 'Not Even Zeus', *Oxford Studies in Ancient Philosophy*, 25 (Winter), 345–61.

Gretenkord, J. C. (1981), *Der Freiheitsbegriff Epiktets*. Bochum: Studienverlag Brockmeyer.

Hadas, M. (1958) (tr.), *Seneca: The Stoic Philosophy of Seneca*. Garden City, NY: Doubleday.

Hadot, P. (1978), 'Une clé des Pensées de Marc Aurèle, les trois topoi philosophiques selon Épictète', *Études philosophique*. Paris: Presses Universitaires, pp. 65–83.

Hijmans, B. L. (1959), ΑΣΚΗΣΙΣ: *Notes on Epictetus' Educational System*. Assen: Van Gorcum.

Inwood, B. (1985), *Ethics and Human Action in Early Stoicism*. New York: Oxford University Press.

—— (1996), 'L' *oikeiosis* sociale chez Épictète', in Algra, van der Horst, and Runia (1996), pp. 243–64.

Ioppolo, A. M. (1980), *Aristone di Chio e lo stoicismo antico*. Napoli: Bibliopolis.

Irwin, T. H. (1986), 'Stoic and Aristotelian Conceptions of Happiness', in Schofield and Striker (1986), pp. 205–44.

Jagu, A. (1946), *Épictète et Platon*. Paris: J. Vrin.

Kahn, C. H. (1988), 'Discovering the Will: From Aristotle to Augustine', in Dillon and Long (1988), pp. 234–59.

Kamtekar, R. (1998), 'ΑΙΔΩΣ in Epictetus', *Classical Philology*, 93 (2), 136–60.

Klauser, T. (1962) (ed.), *Reallexicon für Antike und Christentum*, Vol. 5. Stuttgart: Hiersemann.

Kokolakis, M. (1961), 'Hermeneutics in Epictetus', *Athena*, LXV, 11–24.

Korsgaard, C. M. (1983), 'Two Distinctions in Goodness', *The Philosophical Review*, 92 (April), 169–96.

Laurenti, R. (1966), 'Musonio e Epitteto', *Sophia*, XXXIV, 317–35.

Le Hir, J. (1954), 'Les Fondements Psychologiques et Religieux de la Morale d'Épictète', *Lettres d'Humanité*, XIII (4), 73–93.

Liddell, H. G., Scott, R., and Jones, H. S. (1996), *A Greek–English Lexicon*. Oxford: Oxford University Press.

Long, A. A. (1968), 'Aristotle's Legacy to Stoic Ethics', *Bulletin of the Institute of Classical Studies*, 15, 72–85.

—— (1970–71), 'The Logical Basis of Stoic Ethics', *Proceedings of the Aristotelian Society*, 71, 85–104.

—— (1971) (ed.), *Problems in Stoicism*. London: Athlone Press.

—— (1986), *Hellenistic Philosophy*, 2nd edn. Berkeley: University of California Press.

—— (1996), 'The Socratic Tradition: Diogenes, Crates, and Hellenistic Ethics', in Branham and Goulet-Cazé (1996), pp. 28–46.

—— (2002), *Epictetus: A Stoic and Socratic Guide to Life.* Oxford: Oxford University Press.

—— and Sedley, D. N. (1987), *The Hellenistic Philosophers*, 2 vols. Cambridge: Cambridge University Press.

Martinazzoli, F. (1948), 'Doxarion: i diminutivi nello stile di Epitteto', *La parola del passato*, 3 (9), 262–8.

Merchant, C. (1980), *The Death of Nature: Women, Ecology and the Scientific Revolution.* San Francisco: Harper & Row.

Millar, F. (1965), 'Epictetus and the Imperial Court', *Journal of Roman Studies*, 55, 141–8.

Moreau, J. (1948), 'Ariston et le Stoïcisme', *Revue des Études Anciennes*, 50, 27–48.

—— (1964), 'Épictète ou le secret de la liberté', *Revue de l'Enseignement philosophique*, 34 (4), 3–13.

Moulinier, L. (1964), 'Quelques mots du vocabulaire d'Épictète', *Annales de la Fac. des Lettres d'Aix*, 38, 73–86.

Nakhov, I. M. (1980), 'Épictète et le cynisme', in A. A. Takho-Godi and I. M. Nakhov (eds), *L'image et le mot.* Moskva: Moskva University, pp. 114–32.

Nussbaum, M. C. (1986), *The Fragility of Goodness: Luck and Ethics in Greek Tragedy and Philosophy.* Cambridge: Cambridge University Press.

—— (1994), *The Therapy of Desire: Theory and Practice in Hellenistic Ethics.* Princeton: Princeton University Press.

Oldfather, W. A. (1925/28), *Epictetus: The Discourses as Reported by Arrian, the Manual, and Fragments*, 2 vols. Cambridge, MA: Harvard University Press.

—— (1927), *Contributions toward a Bibliography of Epictetus.* Urbana: University of Illinois Press.

—— (1952), *Contributions toward a Bibliography of Epictetus: A Supplement*, M. Harman (ed.). Urbana: University of Illinois Press.

Pauly, A. F. von and Wissowa, G. (1909) (eds), *Paulys Realencyclopädie der classischen Altertumswissenschaft* (Neue Bearbeitung), 83 vols. Stuttgart: J. B. Metzler, Vol. 6, 126–32.

Pembroke, S. G. (1971), 'oikeiōsis', in Long (1971), pp. 114–48.

Pesce, D. (1939), 'La morale di Epitteto', *Rivista di Filosofia*, 30, 250–64.

Pohlenz, M. (1948), *Die Stoa: Geschichte einer geistigen Bewegung.* Göttingen: Vandenhöck & Ruprecht.

Reale, G. (1985), *The Systems of the Hellenistic Age,* J. R. Catan (ed. and tr.). Albany: State University of New York Press.

—— (1990), *The Schools of the Imperial Age,* J. R. Catan (ed. and tr.). Albany: State University of New York Press.

Reydams-Schils, G. (2005), *The Roman Stoics: Self, Responsibility, and Affection.* Chicago: The University of Chicago Press.

Riondato, E. (1965), *Epitteto.* Milano: Editrice Antenore.

Rist, J. M. (1969), *Stoic Philosophy.* Cambridge: Cambridge University Press.

—— (1978) (ed.), *The Stoics.* Berkeley: University of California Press.

Salomon, A. (1985) (ed.), *Epictetus: The Enchiridion,* T. W. Higginson (tr.). Indianapolis: Bobbs-Merrill.

Sandbach, F. H. (1975), *The Stoics.* London: Chatto & Windus.

Schenkl, H. (1916) (ed.), *Epicteti Dissertationes ab Arriano Digestae,* 2nd edn. Leipzig: Teubner (reprinted Stuttgart, 1965).

Schofield, M. and Striker, G. (1986) (eds), *The Norms of Nature: Studies in Hellenistic Ethics.* Cambridge: Cambridge University Press.

Schweingruber, F. (1943), 'Sokrates und Epiktet', *Hermes,* 78, 52–79.

Seddon, K. (2005), *Epictetus'* Handbook *and the* Tablet of Cebes: *Guides to Stoic Living.* London: Routledge.

Sherman, N. (2005), *Stoic Warriors: The Ancient Philosophy Behind the Military Mind.* Oxford: Oxford University Press.

Sherman, R. R. (1967), 'The Stoic and Education', *Journal of Thought,* 2 (January), 30–41.

Sorabji, R. (2000), *Emotion and Peace of Mind: From Stoic Agitation to Christian Temptation.* Oxford: Oxford University Press.

Souilhé, J. (1949–65), *Épictète: Entretiens,* 4 vols. Paris: 'Les Belles Lettres'.

Spanneut M. (1962), 'Epiktet', in Klauser (1962), pp. 599–681.

—— (1972), 'Épictète chez les moines', *Mélanges de Science Religieuse,* 39, 49–57.

Štajerman, Je. M. (1975), 'Épictète et sa place dans le stoïcisme romain', *Vestnik Drevnej Istorii (Revue d'histoire ancienne)*, 132, 197–210.

Stanton, G. R. (1968), 'The Cosmopolitan Ideas of Epictetus and Marcus Aurelius', *Phronesis*, 13 (2), 183–95.

Starr, C. G. (1949), 'Epictetus and the Tyrant', *Classical Philology*, 44 (1), 20–9.

Stephens, W. O. (1994), 'Stoic Naturalism, Rationalism, and Ecology', *Environmental Ethics*, 16 (3), 275–86.

—— (1996a), *The Ethics of the Stoic Epictetus*. New York: Peter Lang, tr. of Bonhöffer (1894).

—— (1996b), 'Epictetus on How the Stoic Sage Loves', *Oxford Studies in Ancient Philosophy*, 14, 193–210.

—— (1997), 'Epictetus', in J. P. Rodriguez (ed.), *The Historical Encyclopedia of World Slavery*, 2 vols. Santa Barbara, CA: ABC-CLIO Press, p. 258.

—— (1998), Review of *Marcus Aurelius, Meditations*, C. Gill (ed.), R. Hard (tr.), Wordsworth Editions Limited, 1997, *Bryn Mawr Classical Review*, 98.6.23.

—— (2003), Review of Wehner (2000) and of Long (2002), *Ancient Philosophy*, 23 (Fall), 472–81.

—— (2005), 'Marcus Aurelius', in P. O'Grady (ed.), *Meet the Philosophers of Ancient Greece*. Aldershot, England: Ashgate, pp. 211–13.

—— and Feezell, R. (2004), 'The Ideal of the Stoic Sportsman', *The Journal of the Philosophy of Sport*, 31 (2), 196–211.

Stockdale, J. B. (1978), 'The World of Epictetus: Reflections on Survival and Leadership', *The Atlantic Monthly*, 241 (4), 98–106.

Striker, G. (1983), 'The Role of *Oikeiosis* in Stoic Ethics', *Oxford Studies in Ancient Philosophy*, 1, 145–67.

Szumska, D. (1964), 'Epiktet o przyjazni', *Filomata*, 183, 174–83.

Voelke, A.-J. (1973), *L'idée de volonté dans le stoïcisme*. Paris: Presses Universitaires de France.

Wehner, B. (2000), *Die Dialogstruktur in Epiktets Diatriben*. Stuttgart: Franz Steiner.

White, N. P. (1979), 'The Basis of Stoic Ethics', *Harvard Studies in Classical Philology*, 83, 143–78.

White, N. P. (1985) (tr.), *Epictetus: The Handbook of Epictetus.* Indianapolis: Hackett.

Wirth, Th. (1967), 'Arrians Erinnerungen an Epiktet', *Museum Helveticum*, 24, 149–89, 197–216.

Xenakis, I. (1968), 'Logical Topics in Epictetus', *Southern Journal of Philosophy*, 6 (Summer), 94–102.

—— (1969), *Epictetus: Philosopher-therapist.* The Hague: Martinus Nijhoff.

Index

Made in the USA
Coppell, TX
14 June 2020